WE ARE MADE FOR COOPERATION — MARCUS AURELIUS M.D. 161

Aug. 1~ 19~~

Charles A. Black~~

THE MERRY OLD MOBILES

This is copy number .16.4. of
a special autographed edition.

TO MY WIFE
in memory of
Old Car Times

INTRODUCTION TO SPECIAL COLLECTOR'S EDITION

by D. Cameron Peck, President
Antique Automobile Club of America

The marked interest of our generation in how we got to be what we are—we Americans with our gadgets which have reshaped the world both for good and for ill—finds fresh expression in this book about the motor car. Those of us who have made a hobby (and what a rewarding hobby it is!) out of collecting and restoring early automobiles, or, as is the case with Dr. Larry Freeman, collecting the catalogs, cartoons and periodicals dealing with motor car's early days, will not be too surprised at the romantic panorama here unfolded of the motor car's first six decades, but it will not be so for the average reader.

We enthusiasts have long ago abandoned ourselves with unequivocal delight to this cult of the motor car in all its many forms. Some of us—the more bookish sort—collect like Dr. Freeman; others, true antiquarians these, will have nothing built since 1900 and feel that motor cars constructed after 1905 show distinct evidences of that declining civilization announced to us by Oswald Spengler.

At the opposite end of this delightful automotive insanity of ours are the lovers of sports cars, preferably foreign and fascinating, but always fast—a standing mile in how many seconds sort of thing! In between come fanciers of every sort of four wheeled self-propelled vehicle ever conceived, including, of course, those helpless souls with the dreadful gleam in their eyes—the steam car fiends. But perhaps most pitiable of all are those in whom the disease has run its full course. No kind or age of motor car remains unsampled by these men. They become emotionally unbalanced, just as easily over a Willoughby bodied Duesenberg engine No. J-596 ("One of the very last ones, old boy!") as over a 1891 Panhard. Among such are James Melton, Austin Clark, Lindley Bothwell, George Waterman—to mention only a few—and yours truly.

Yes, we have known the motor car for all that it is and have vicariously relived the days and re-experienced the passions of the early motorists herein so engagingly portrayed. For us car collectors, Dr. Freeman does what we have been far too absorbed to do ourselves. For the public at large he does what they never quite realized needed doing. He reminds all of us that the motor car, that device of man's contriving which more than any other has altered the face of the earth and the course of human history, has not only been the instrument of our destiny but in its development presents a story of unsurpassed excitement and romance which we are just beginning to see in its true perspective.

Chicago, Ill., 1949   D. Cameron Peck

The Merry Old Mobiles

By
Larry Freeman

Century House

WATKINS GLEN, NEW YORK

LITHO IN U.S.A.
by BEURMANN-MARSHALL, INC.
Lansing, Michigan

Contents

Preface

I don't recall when I began collecting literature of old cars. Having grown up with the automobile, the subject has always held fascination. Herein I have tried to give a brief illustrated history of the amazing creation whose coming so changed our American way of life. It has come all the way from mechanic's nightmare to rich man's toy to general necessity in the span of one lifetime. Profound social and economic changes have followed its wake. But the subject has its lighter side, too, and this is not overlooked.

I am deeply indebted to individuals and to automobile concerns for aid in making this record possible. Especial credit is due Mrs. Charles Beaumont and Mr. Thomas McKean, whose collections of old-car literature have supplemented my own. The matter of reproduction courtesies I have tried to handle by credit lines on the pictures themselves. Some concerns are out of business. But wherever possible, permission for inclusion was sought and obtained.

I am indebted to Mr. D. Cameron Peck, President of the Antique Automobile Club of America, for a critical reading of the manuscript. Interpretations, however, are quite my own and no claim is made for their definitive character. The life and times of the automobile are still too close for full perspective. All we can now do is look back with nostalgia, recalling something of how far and fast we have come.

I hope you enjoy reading of cars as I enjoyed the writing.

The Freeman Farms   Larry Freeman
July 1, 1949

CHAPTER I

18

95

Get a Horse....

W HEN the automobile made its first appearance in America, it was almost laughed off the streets. Everywhere it was greeted with derision and mirth. If the driver got his vehicle to propel itself even a few short blocks, little wonder was expressed for this marvel of applied science. Instead, there were loud guffaws over its weird appearance and erratic movement, howls of protest over its stinking smoke and ear-splitting noise. Whenever the word was passed that the "crazy contraption" was on the street again, people ran out of their houses and waited expectantly for the fun to begin. As the thing lurched into view they nudged each other and tittered genteelly, after the manner of the day; and as the motor died with a sickening cough and the driver climbed down to begin his futile cranking the cry went up "Get a Horse."

In those early days, no one gave the automobile an outside chance of becoming a major necessity of the American way of life, let alone its possibilities for pleasure. Its inventors were regarded as crackpots—in a class with those who talked of riding a rocket to Mars; its drivers as exhibitionists and mechanical perverts addicted to "bad taste."

The complete skepticism of America towards the future of the motor car is revealed by a typical incident of the Gay Nineties. Seeking capital to develop his patent for a self-propelled gasoline motor vehicle, George Seldon told a friend they would both live to see more horseless than horsedrawn carriages on the streets of their home town, Rochester, N. Y.

1. Mr. Podger: Oh, papa's little man mustn't cry. Dobbin was old and useless and Mr. Hawpatch will take good care of him. Now we'll go for a grand ride in a new automobile.

2. The Man: Now don't forget, Colonel. Forward, ahead she goes; back, backwards it goes. Mr. Podgers: Very well, my man, stand aside and we're off.

3. The Man: Push her forward. FORWARD, I say!

4. Mr. Hawpatch: Now, what could that noise be, Dobbin?

5. Mr. Podgers: My poor dears, how we have suffered to get here.

6. Mr. Podgers: Yes, Mr. Howpatch, and you can have that, that automobile, too!

This prospect was too much for the prospect to take. He said, "George, you're crazy, give me my money back."

Nor is this all. When a Detroit merchant was finally induced to put up some money for Ford, the news so worried his coal jobber in Cleveland that the latter made a special trip to Detroit and insisted on an audit of the man's books to safeguard himself against loss. Interest in automobiles was tantamount to a declaration of insanity and loss of sound business sense. Why put money into a product sure to be met with raucous laughter. Get a Horse!

Belles as well as business men turned their backs upon the early horseless carraige. Should a progressive swain appear at the door in such a vehicle, his lady love would likely send down word that she was indisposed. To ride so publicly amid smoke and noise was considered indelicate. More courageous and experimental members of the fair sex were held back by Mama's disapproval. And if a couple defied convention it was well to choose a populated route, so as to avoid "Compromising" the young lady due to breakdown in out of the way places. Newstories of the period strongly hint of shotgun weddings where this precaution was ignored.

It was common practice for the early two seaters to be occupied only by men, one facing forward and watching the road, the other facing backward and watching over the motor.

What a sight this must have made. At best, the first autos looked for all the world like an open buggy, complete even to whip and whip socket. Some did not have bodies at all, merely a buggy seat mounted on a frame. There were no fenders, no hood and dash, no covered top, nothing that now has become synonymous with car design. Their dubious charms were even more questionable when considered mechanically. The single cylinder gas engine was mounted over the rear wheels and power was transmitted by a sprocket and chain, as in bicycles. Steering was accomplished by means of a tiller. Brakes were primitive and often failed on a steep down grade. There were no lights and no instrument panel as we know it today. The motor car was made to "perco-

12

"Stop that tooting before we call a constable. What's the idea trying to make deliveries in that infernal thing! Get a Horse!"

"Sorry, sir, but the thing's beyond me. Better leave her here and get a horse."

Early automobiles were converted carriages. Top to bottom: De-Tamble Miller air cooled, Schacht chain drive cranked from rear, from which the expression "twist her tail," and Holsom rope drive. J. B. Van Sciver collection.

late" only with the greatest effort. First it had to be primed, then the cylinder pet cock had to be opened to drain off excess gasoline, then the spark might be adjusted, then one cranked and cranked, primed, drained, readjusted, and cranked some more, usually to the accompaniment of sidewalk cries to, "twist her tail harder."

Drivers were usually well begrimed before they got their mechanical steed under way. And the best guarantee of seeing it back in the barn safely was a goodly supply of spare parts and tools. Frequent and unpredictable stops were the order of the day. One early driver remarked that he learned to see the city streets from a new angle—laying under the car and looking up! Get a horse!

Few ventured to drive these first cars out into the country. Roads were impassable with horse drawn vehicles sometimes stalled by mud up to the axle. The average person traveled only within a radius of eight miles from home.

Gradually, however, as more and more people were induced—often most reluctantly—to "go for a spin", summer trips into the country side became quite popular. The rigors of this kind of entertainment were well covered by cartoon comment of the day. It is reliably reported that many car owners found a good use for the whip that came with the early auto body—to drive the cows off the road or if the motor failed, one could use the whip on some horses hired to tow the vehicle home. Here, of course, was the best of all reasons for the slogan of the age—Get a Horse!

And how was Dobbin faring in all this? To say the least, he would have none of it. Farmers driving to church now had to cope with runaway horses that had been frightened out of their wits by the Sunday excursionists. So loud was the clamor that one inventor, Uriah Smith of Battle Creek, Michigan sought to obviate the dangers of frightened horses by designing an auto body the front portion of which terminated in the shape of a horse's head and neck. "This expedient," he claimed, "by having the appearance of a horse, would raise no fears in any skittish animal; for the live horse would be thinking of another horse approaching, and before he could discover his error and see that he was fooled, the strange carriage would have passed, and it would then be too late to grow frantic and fractious." The inventor also recommended his device as a windbreak and a receptacle for gasoline.

Less conservative souls did not think all this necessary. A New York paper soothed its readers with the following report: "A motor car has been in operation on the streets of our fair city for a week and is apparently a success. It has not balked at the steep hills, run away, or backed over the curbing. No property damage, direct or indirect, has been caused and it seems our people and horses will both grow acclimated to this new invention."

Who were the makers of these new contraptions—these horseless carriages that were to change completely the social habits of America? Five "firsts," stand out. One name, Ford, is synonymous with the industrial progress of America. The other four names have sunk into oblivion. Yet there are some still among us who may recall when these other four names all but eclipsed the name of Ford. Who were they?

Charles E. Duryea made the first gas powered automobile to run on the roads in America, out in Springfield, Massachusetts in 1892. Ford's experimental gas car ran in 1893 and Elwood Haynes had his going in Kokomo in 1894. Steam and electric powered vehicles were running shortly before this time, but the dangers of expanding steam and the costs of heavy storage batteries turned most experimental minds toward the gas-driven buggy. Ransom E. Olds, who made a steam car in 1891, produced his first gas-powered vehicle in 1897. Alexander Winton got his under motion in 1895.

These five men, Duryea, Ford, Haynes, Olds, and Winton, launched the automobile in America. Yet not one of them can be said to have invented it. Each worked independently, without knowledge of the others problems or help from the other's experiences. Each was a mechanic at heart, with little

16

George Seldon received first American patent for gas buggy but was years in getting this one built to his specifications.

Meanwhile, the machine shop assembled cars of men like Elwood Haynes were already driving foreign car competition off the streets of America.

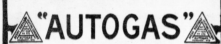

initial interest in anything beyond the primary purpose of making his creation work. Not one of them had heard of George Seldon, of Rochester, New York who had a patent for a gas-propelled vehicle yet to be built and whose lawsuits came to involve the whole industry. Not one of these five men, in the experimental 90's, even imagined that he was founding an industry. At least one of them is on record as worried lest the endurance of steam cars, like the Stanley and the White, and the reliability of the electrics for city transportation would leave for the gas buggy no field of successful competition. Yet the days of ascendency of steamers and electrics was comparatively brief. By the end of the decade, gasoline had become the lifeblood of the automobile industry And so, to the five men who first showed America how to use gas power effectively must go the name of "pioneer". To Ford alone, of course, fell the accident of power and wealth.

The student of social history marvels a little that an invention producing such profound changes in American living was—and still is—referred to by proper names. When we say we are leaving the house, do we say we are taking the auto? No, it is the Ford, the Buick or the Packard. If we discuss a friend's possesion, do we mention his motor car? No, it is his Chevrolet or Studebaker. No one speaks of the light bulb as the Edison, the radio as a Deforest, a television set as a Dumont. Nor does the reason for this lie in the clever brains of advertising copy writers. There has always been something intensely personal about an automobile. From the first, the basic parts—wheels, gears, motors—were available to anyone who wished to try his hand at assembly. And the cars that worked had the impress of personal assembly upon them. Even after the creation of mass assembly lines, drivers gained confidence from the thought that the builder stood personally behind his product. Certainly in the early days, the auto became a thing personified—the alter ego of its maker. Cars, in fact, were first marketed largely in terms of the exploits of their makers.

And such exploits!

There was Charles E. Duryea, whose car won the first automobile race run in America. This was promoted in 1895 by the Chicago Times-Herald with a first prize of $2,000, for completing the lake-front circuit from Jackson Park to Evanston and return, about 52 miles. Duryea made it at an average speed of seven and one-half miles an hour, with frequent time-out for various checkups and engine trouble. He raced against five other machines, including a "Rodgers machine" entered by R. H. Macy and Company of New York, a "Motor Drag," "Electrobat," "Sturgis Electric" and an imported "Benz machine"—this last the only other car to make the complete circuit. Haynes and Apperson started their car for the Jackson Park takeoff, but threw a tire on the way in avoiding a street car, so gave up the idea of racing. Duryea performed his miracle by throwing slush from the city streets over his engine to keep it from overheating. Umpires riding with him reported the following time delays in minutes: "By sparking machine failure, 2 minutes; by loss of tire, 7 minutes; by adjusting tire second time, 3 minutes; by sparking machine trouble, 2 minutes; by taking water, 4 minutes; by sparking machine, 2 minutes; losing route, 4 minutes; taking water, 3 minutes; taking water, 4 minutes; total loss of time, 31 minutes."

Duryea next won the 1896 Memorial Day race from New York City Hall to Irvington on the Hudson, and, later the same year, the first international race in England. He had now beaten the world record.

Showmanship gaining ascendency over sound business practice, Duryea took his Buggeat on tour with Barnum and Bailey's Circus and let the manufacture of cars at Springfield go to pot. His one big chance came when Colonel Pope, head of the largest bicycle company in America, offered to manufacture the Buggeat on a royalty basis. This would have been a natural connection, for bicycles were the popular self-propelled vehicles of the day and were making people conscious of their wretched roads and the need for improving transportation. Duryea was interested and suggested a royalty of

Automobileer Duryea thought to popularize his gas powered creation by parading with Barnum and Bailey's freaks, as shown in this old circus poster.

The Stanley Brothers also appeared at public gatherings with their steam powered autobuggy, much to the consternation of Dobbin.

$50.00 for every car sold. Pope offered only $5.00, arguing that Duryea had no new invention, "simply an engine set on two bicycles connected by a steel frame." Duryea thought different and the project collapsed. His brother Frank, however, went into a combine to produce the Stevens-Duryea.

Likewise there was Elwood Haynes. In 1894 a car built to his specifications by the Apperson Brothers in their Kokomo, Indiana, machine shop attracted considerable attention. With the public distracted by such events as the Chicago World's Fair, the panic of '93, the Klondyke gold rush and the Spanish-American war, few Haynes-Appersons were sold. Haynes' chief interest seems to have been in a quality custom built job. Crowded out of the company by the Apperson's in 1900, he joined with Duryea in tilting for the title of auto pioneer. Meanwhile other hands took up the torch of accomplishment and production.

Alexander Winton, a bicycle manufacturer in Cleveland, is usually credited with having made the first commercial sale of an automobile, in 1897. Although this "first" was hotly contested by Haynes, Winton certainly deserves a great deal of credit for taking his model back from the dissatisfied customer and making a long cross-country trip in it to prove its worth. The only concrete result of the publicity attending his trip was an offer to travel in a circus parade,—an offer which Winton turned down in disgust.

It is hard to realize that in the '90's the auto was taken seriously only by a few experimentally minded mechanics and that the public's major delight was to see it exhibit its shortcomings. The majority of Americans now over sixty saw their first motor car at the circus. By accident or intent, it frequently broke down and had to be towed into the lot behind the lion wagon. The mockery of rustics and townfolk alike was finally too much for Winton. He was the first man to make advertising copy by reversing the order of the circus parade attraction. When he saw some wag dragging his latest car through the streets with a placard saying no one could operate it without the aid of horses, he smarted for vengeance. A few hours later, another Winton car followed the same route as the parade, dragging behind it a farm cart in which appeared a dejected looking donkey and a placard saying "the only animal who is unable to drive a Winton." Understandably enough, this kind of horse play helped sell cars.

Ransom E. Olds was also advertising conscious. Flushed with the seeming dependability of his first successful gasoline buggy, he adopted the slogan "nothing to watch but the road." This proved a little premature, for a widely quoted remark of a disgusted Oldsmobile owner was "I get dammed tired of watching the same piece of road." Undaunted, Olds continued to improve his creation until he had a very roadable little runabout and a factory organization to produce it by the hundreds rather than singly as heretofore. A tremendous stimulus was given to popular interest by the Olds cross country trip, from Detroit to New York in five days. The driver's luggage was a box of parts most likely to break under the jolts and poundings of unkept roads, the stresses and strains of chuckholes, ruts and rocks. One cannot imagine the condition of roads in those days. The average country highway was scarcely more than a trail that wound between the fences. Roads took their serpentine way, going around trees, dodging low spots, following any little ridge or elevation. They were, in fact, the path of least resistance. On the Olds cross country run, New York State roads became so bad that the driver was forced to take to the Erie canal towpath, where he disputed the right of way with the mule teams attached to the canal boats. Always the little six hundred pound machine had to jump the tow rope, for the teamsters would not have their mules where they might stampede toward the water. But the Oldsmobile hurdled this and other obstructions, so that the driver could take his machine triumphantly down Fifth Avenue and into the newly organized New York Automobile Show.

Meanwhile, there was Henry Ford. Quietly in his backyard machine shop he had been making and testing auto-

26

MOTOR-CAR ACCESSORIES

Clothing for motor vehicle users possesses as its most important character-istics the qualities of keeping out dust and wet. Leather garments (Figs. 85 and 86), because of their impenetrability to dirt, and, in many cases of specially-tanned goods, to water, are much favored. Waterproof woven fabrics, however, are lighter, and by many considered neater in appearance, for which reason their vogue is great.

Other apparel, ranging from gloves to goggles, is of obvious necessity to the motor vehicle user who would be comfortable under all conditions.

Goggles (Fig. 87) and *face masks* (Fig. 88), which afford perfect protection from dust, wind, and the glare of an unduly bright day, are oftentimes absolutely essential. Many remarkably light though rarely becoming devices of this sort are to be had.

Fig. 85.—Leather Suit

Fig. 87.--Goggles

Fig. 88.— Mask

Fig. 89.—Poncho

Fig. 90.—Foot-Bag Lap Robe

Fig. 86.—Leather Coat

Figs. 91, 92 and 93.—Tire Pumps

Gloves are imperative in cold weather, when the hands are exposed to all the severity of wind and storm, with a minimum of exercise to keep them warm. Gloves with ample gauntlets, to cover the opening of the sleeve, or with separate gauntlets for the same purpose, are the best.

Veils, for women, not only of a mesh fine enough to afford protection to the eyes and the complexion, but also of an ample size to secure the headgear, are useful.

Lap Robes, and bag-like *foot muffs,* of fur (Fig. 90) are very comfortable. For very cold weather, footwarmers, in which briquettes of a peat-like fuel will burn smokelessly and

mobiles,—a fanatic bent on the sole purpose of making the machine practical. This, apparently, is the background for the so-called Ford myth. This myth conceives Henry as inspired in his youth with the vision of a light, strong, simple, efficient automobile available at low cost to the entire population. The myth goes on to hold that Henry struggled to this one end through thick and thin until he became the greatest industrialist of the age and the founder of the world's largest private fortune. It does not take anything from Henry Ford's great achievement that the facts tell a somewhat different story. He actually spent his first 10 years in turning out 5 automobiles, and not until after fifteen years of work on expensive models K and 9 9 9 racing cars, did he create the basis for the famed low-priced model T. Ford's early progress was slow compared to other makers, not because he was so sure of the way he should do, rather because he was so unsure. Only once do we find him in the early auto news, and this pre-1900 report of a "Ride with Henry" carries no mention of how useful his creation was likely to be. The quotation below is in the best Sunday-supplement manner and shows how little was really known of the automobile in those early days. The reporter tells about the thrills of his experience rather than about what made the machine go.

'Mr. Ford, the automobileer, began by giving his steed three or four sharp jerks at the right side of the seat—in order, he said to drive the charge of air and gasoline into the exploding cylinder — with incomparable swiftness the machine picked up its speed and glided into the snowy, wind-blown street.. The puffing of the engine assumed a higher key. She was flying along at eight miles an hour.. "Hold on tight," said Ford, "when we strike the asphalt we will have a run."

"How fast?"

"Twenty-five miles an hour."

"Hold on, I'll get out."

Bang! bang! That was the warning bell under the seat. Whiz.. she picked up speed with infinite rapidity. As she

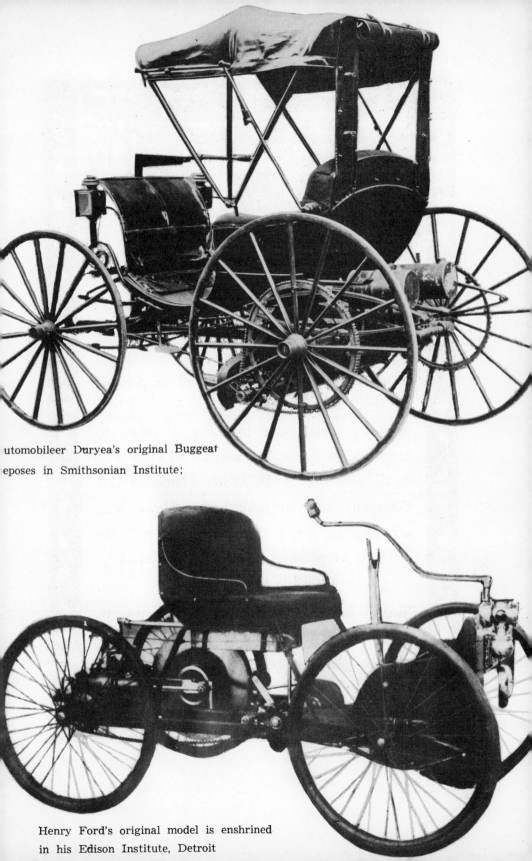

utomobileer Duryea's original Buggeat
eposes in Smithsonian Institute;

Henry Ford's original model is enshrined
in his Edison Institute, Detroit

1901

BUY A SKENE,

A successful steam automobile built by reliable makers, and enjoy the fascination of a horseless carriage. We will be pleased to demonstrate the many points of superiority which our machine possesses to any one who is interested. There is a small amount of **TREASURY STOCK** in this Company still unsubscribed. Those who are looking for a "good thing" will do well to correspond with me immediately.

ARTHUR C. EDDY, Treasurer

Skene American Automobile Company

Carr Bldg., Harrison Ave., Springfield, Mass.

Denied access to Wall Street financing, early car companies tried to sell. stock direct to automobile enthusiasts.

rushed on, there was a clattering behind—the new noise of the automobile... I began to have a creepy feeling and told Ford I wanted to get out. "Nonsense," he replied, "No danger.. I'll wager that a race horse cannot be hauled up in less than one minute, but we'll do it in six feet.." With that the automobileer pushed something, and with the suddenness of complete collapse, the steed came to a standstill.'

Such free advertising was not enough to sell Fords. Compared with Winton, who now had the title of national track champion, and Olds, who was about ready for quantity production of his curved dash runabout, Ford lagged far behind in the public eye. He had, however, built a two cylinder motor at a time when other manufacturers were still making one cylinder models. With this, he challenged Winton to a ten mile race,—and won.

A contemporary account of that race meet, where steam and gasoline vehicles competed, each in its own class, gives an entertaining picture of public reaction to the motor car fifty years ago. Here we find first mention of auto racing as a sport, with wonder still expressed that these horseless buggies would run at all.

"That a crowd of ten thousand should turn out on a day so cheerless proves the interest there is in this new sport... a lively five-mile race for steam machines opened the p r o-gramme... This was followed by a race in which Mr. Ford beat all comers."

Ford's accomplishment was widely publicized, and for some time thereafter his energies were given to the development of racing cars rather than to the utilitarian creations later to become synonymous with his name. In fact, of the five 'firsts' in automobile history, only Olds caught at once the vision of a practical car for the average man's purse. Ford, Winton, Haynes and Duryea concentrated on speed and more speed, until by the turn of the century cars could go faster than their drivers were willing to travel.

In their desire for the free publicity attending new speed records, early car manufacturers combed the country for dare-

The automobile at St. Louis Fair, a 1904 cartoon by McCutcheon

The automobile arrives in Bird City, Ill., a cartoon by McCutcheon

STYLE SAFETY COMFORT

Pope *Waverley* ELECTRIC

THE STANHOPE, PRICE $1,500

Study this handsome Carriage for a moment, and you will understand why it is one of the most popular models we make.

THE STANHOPE, among electric vehicles, is the acme of good form. It embodies, more than any type, not only style and safety, but the desirable virtues of ease and convenience as well.

Do you fully understand how much you can depend upon a Pope-Waverley electric? Do you realize that it is virtually immune from disabling accidents?

The operation of the Pope-Waverley electric is simplicity itself. Simply turn on the power and steer. Always ready, free from dirt, noise, odor or vibration.

We make Runabouts, Chelseas, Coupes, Physicians, Road, Station. Delivery Wagons and Trucks to Specifications.

Pope Motor Car Co.,
Waverley Dept.   -   INDIANAPOLIS, IND.

We exhibit in New York at Madison Square Garden only, January 12th to 19th.

devil drivers. Typical of this group was Barney Oldfield, who first won fame on the bicycle race-tracks. He had never driven an automobile until Ford hired him to pilot his new 999 racer . Over a week of thrills in learning, Oldfield developed such speed that the 999 could not be controlled by the one hand tiller typical of early design. With a two-hand steering contraption and great quantities of nerve, however, Barney Oldfield was soon launched and on his way to becoming a legendary figure in early auto racing.

Early emphasis on racing and racers did not obscure to some men, the possibilities of a utilitarian car. This was particularly true for steam and electric vehicles. Both these unsung types of early automobiling deserve much credit for putting a solid groundwork of popular demand under the new mode of travel.

Electric vehicles operated by storage batteries were developed in America as early as 1891. At the time of the World's Fair, a Chicago paper reported "The sight of a well loaded carriage moving majestically along the street with no horse in front and with apparently nothing on board to give it motion has been almost too much for the eye to believe . . . police have to clear a way to keep the curious from interrupting its passage." The next few years of this decade saw electrics on city streets in ever increasing numbers. Because of their slow speed and ease of operation, these became in time the accepted town car for ladies. Men might mount the gasoline demons, but for women the electric alone was considered safe and sane.

Steam cars, notably the Stanley and the White, also began to capture popular fancy in terms of their early dependability over gasoline vehicles. In operation on American roads before the gas powered auto, they often yielded the right of way on starts, but once in motion gave little trouble. Credit for practicality and dependability goes mainly to the Stanley brothers and their little Stanley Steamer. When this first appeared on the streets of Newton, Massachusetts, in

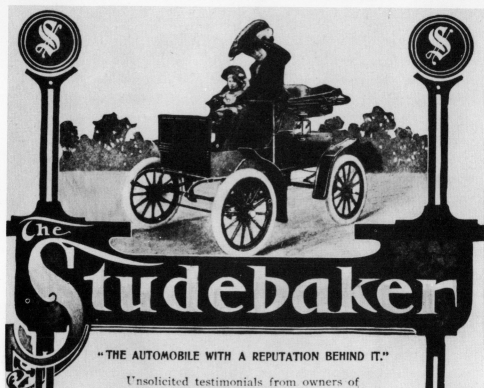

The Studebaker

No Accidents with
The Oldsmobile

Mechanical skill and mathematical exactness eliminate the danger of the horse's uncertain temper, sudden fright and unruly disposition—no "Runaways" with *"The Best Thing on Wheels."*

The controlling mechanism is simple, strong and instantly responsive to the will of the driver, giving a sense of perfect security. There is no factor of uncertainty in the Oldsmobile—*"Nothing to watch but the road."*

Price $650.00

Equipped with a motor, running 30 miles on one gallon of gasolene, an improved mixer which guarantees a uniform charge and perfect explosion every time, and strong trussed axles. Call on any of our 58 Selling Agencies or write for illustrated book to Dept. D.

Olds Motor Works
Detroit, Mich.

1897, the first horse that saw it broke the whiffletrees and ran four miles before it was stopped. What a sight this "tea-kettle on wheels" must have been. A two seated buggy box complete with leather dash, whipsocket and all, set on over-size bicycle tires, guided by a man with whiskers and a derby hat, his exact counterpart seated beside him and watching the boiler spout steam. As the Stanley brothers showed off their creation at various horseless carriage meets and carried off honor after honor, curiosity turned to craving for many. People who had at first laughed at these little teakettles. secretly began to covet one for their very own. The Stanley's made a number of dependable cars in those early years and sold them. Other competitors appeared, chiefly the White, a hobby outgrowth for the president of the White Sewing Machine Company of Cleveland. Its boiler was mounted under the hood, whereas the Stanley had the engine over the rear axle. All steam cars showed roadability from the first,—once the steam was up. After you lighted the kerosene burner under the boiler you had to sit and wait for about twenty minutes. This seems to have been the steamers chief draw-back to widespread fancy, a difficulty which might have been remedied had more ingenuity been utilized. If Henry Ford, or General Motors Kettering had been steam engineers instead of gas buggy addicts, American cars might today be powered by steam instead of by gasoline. As it was, one early steam-man, R. E. Olds, finding greater promise in gasoline combustion, had by the end of the century, a workable plan for mass production of a roadable motor car, the Oldsmobile Runabout.

The public was about ready to adopt the automobile as something that had come to stay. No longer was it sneered at. Its drivers were beginning to be looked upon with some envy rather than as "squirrels." Traffic laws came into being to regulate its speed on city streets, eight miles an hour in New York being a record for tolerance. In Boston, the city fathers passed a law that excluded automobiles from the streets between the hours of 10:30 A. M. and 9 P. M. And in Newark, N. J., city officials ruled that an automobile was subject to

GROUT TOURING MODEL

We make Tonneaus and Light, Frenchy Steam Cars also

GROUT BROS.   ORANGE, MASS

THE WHITE
STEAM CARRIAGE

AN ABSOLUTELY CLEAN RECORD

being one of two out of seventy entries to achieve this distinction.

The conditions of this run were unusually severe, the competing vehicles being required to make five separate journeys over different routes, and submit to brake contests and hill climbing trials.

The WHITE STEAM CARRIAGE used was a six horse=power vehicle taken from stock, and not only scored

1,800 POINTS OUT OF A POSSIBLE 1,800

but demonstrated its fuel economy by using only 13 quarts per day.

WHITE SEWING MACHINE CO., CLEVELAND, OHIO
(AUTOMOBILE DEPARTMENT)

22 Union Square, New York, N. Y. 300 Post Street, San Francisco, Cal. 12 Woodward Avenue, Detroit, Mich.
509 Tremont Street, Boston, Mass. 609 Main Street, Buffalo, N. Y. 300 Rose Building, Cleveland, Ohio.

the same traffic laws as a traction engine and must be preceded by a watch an eighth of a mile in advance.

Such hampering restrictions naturally took the experimental motorists out into the country, where roads were all but impassable. They did not stay that way for long. Motorists agreed to pay a tax on their vehicles only if the money was used to fix the roads. The lobbying that went on for more and better highways is as much a story of the automobile's progress as are the cars themselves. Today's highest priced Lincoln or Cadillac could get stuck in the mud just as quickly today as could the cars of fifty years ago. Chuckholes no longer exist because enough people got mad and demanded that something be done. It was all well and good to laugh at the antics of a stalled car from the sidelines; but when you became its owner, the matter ceased to be a joke. That, more than anything else, may explain the passing of the cry—Get a Horse!

THE FIRST AMERICAN AUTOMOBILE LEGISLATION (SPEED LIMIT 12 MILES PER HOUR - 8 MILES IN CITY) ENACTED AT HARTFORD IN 1901.

All the leading varieties of motor cars were exhibited in this first Automobile Show held in New York in 1901. Almost a third of the floor space was taken up by various electric cars and most of the rest by steam cars. The gasoline car had almost no representation, yet within ten years it had crowded out its contenders for popularity. Not a single steering is visible and body design is still in the horseless carriage stage. There are no remaining examples of some of the cars shown, and of others not even a hub-cap survives. Contrast the clutter with today's streamlined Automobile Show.

CHAPTER II

19

05

Rich Man's Fancy...

THE year 1905 saw the automobile well launched in the favor of the rich. Although Olds was out with a practical car for only six hundred and sixty dollars, hardly a farmer or modest business man then expected to own one of these noisy, smoke belching, hard riding vehicles. Among the wealthy, however, the motor car was a new found toy, regardless of whether they paid six hundred or six thousand for their fun. The amateur sporting element, which in those days meant mainly the smart social set, had been made automobile conscious by the numerous races held around the country. They did not care much for backroads touring, but driving around well paved city streets was something any dandy could readily negotiate. Largely because New York had more paving and more rich men than any other city, this now became the center of the infant motor industry. Manufacturers from Massachusetts to Kokomo, Indiana, found here a ready market for any car their feeble resources could produce. Along with foreign car makers, they took Broadway showrooms, from where salesmen trundled their samples into the street for driving demonstrations. Thus was Automobile Row born, in enough noise and stench to give even the cleft-chin Arrow-collar man and the well poised Gibson Girl a splitting headache. Still they came, these fashion plates of yesteryear, lured by a strange fascination to have one of these twentieth century marvels for their very own. Interest was chiefly in racing one's own car against his friends, and incidentally in keeping up with the Astors, the Vanderbilts, and the Jones next door.

44

JILTED! W. O. Wilson's famed cartoon, 1904 Judge

"End of the Road" by Pabst and
"Climb into the Clouds" by Helck.
Reprinted from Esquire, Copyr'd 1946

No one yet thought of making business trips in it; trains were for that purpose, automobiles for a few hours of play.

The automobile got its big start towards society sponsorship in 1900, when William K. Vanderbilt, Jr., drove his new car all the way from Newport, Rhode Island, to New York City for a summer lark. "Automobile Topics," one of the first publications devoted exclusively to the new activity, contains this authoritative note on what the well dressed motorist wore on such a trip:

"Mr. Vanderbilt presented a novel appearance when he arrived in this city at eleven o'clock at night. He was attired in leather jacket, large goggles over his eyes and a patent leather cap . . . Accompanying him was his French chauffeur and a footman . . . Mrs. Vanderbilt, who had left Newport by train, had waited all day at the Waldorf-Astoria for him . . . Mr. Vanderbilt took no account of his miles per hour, for he was delayed by rain and going much out of his way by not knowing the roads . . . his costume showed the effect of muddy travel, but was quickly furbished by the footman before his appearance in the Waldorf . . . He thinks his fastest time was at about forty miles an hour."

The Vanderbilt saga was widely quoted in society news columns. Other socially prominent persons took up with cars, and even began to take them out into the country-side on endurance trials. Whereas previously a fine carriage and pair were looked upon as the proper equipage of wealth and position, many socialites now saw in the automobile, particularly the lovely looking foreign makes, a far greater eclat. By driving them, they could show their superiority to convention, set a new mode. By chancing the rigors of cross country driving (with the chauffeur along to help with repairs), they proved their courage and daring. Newspapers of the day made a great thing of the social acceptability of the automobile. They cooed over the fact that "women like Mrs. Herman Oelrichs and Mrs. Wm. K. Vanderbilt, who are noted for taking up sports which have the merit of unconventionality, will not be satisfied until they have driven their motor carriages through the city streets . . . while their husbands show even greater daring by engaging one another in hill climbs and cross-county races.'' When the news leaked out that Mrs. Stuyvesant Fish planned to drive her new motor carriage to a Newport party, the tone was set for her followers in the ''400,'' to say nothing of countless climbers who saw in a glittering, expensive, powerful sounding motor car a badge of social merit. All over the country the horse was now old hat, at least as a conveyance for the social elite. In 1904, two million dollars were paid out for foreign cars—the first to carry that look of necessary swank. By 1905, however, American manufacturers had caught on, selling shiny expensive domestic makes to the tune of three million dollars or more than was previously spent on foreign cars of this class. The reason for the shift of social preference to American cars has been variously explained. Some stress increasing American mechanical competence. This, no doubt, had its effect. But even more important was the American genius for making cars look expensive, when they were not. Not all the social climbers could afford a Daimler or a Rolls Royce, and when an American make like the Locomobile came along looking just as exclusive there was no reason to look for something else. Furthermore, by almost imperceptible degrees, the various American cars were graded down until one who could not afford a Locomobile could have a Cadillac that looked almost as good, and one that could not afford a Cadillac could get its near cousin in a Buick, or if the Buick was still too much, could still have almost the same thing in the little Oldsmobile Runabout. Quite early it became car rather than what car that marked the social elect. More and more people gravitated to the little Oldsmobile, not necessarily because it was so relatively cheap as because, of all makes advertised in the popular magazines of the day, it alone had a mass assembly line and could come somewhere near to filling the orders that flowed in. Olds turned out over three thousand cars in 1905, when his competitors were counting output by the hundreds or less.

When Gus Edwards wrote his popular song, ''In My

Cars

RIGHT THROUGH THE YEAR

1905 JAN

Merry Oldsmobile," he little thought that he was establishing a social institution across the whole countryside; and when Chauncey Depew drove down Fifth Avenue at the tiller of an Oldsmobile this jolly little popular priced car received the ultimate stimulus of snobbery. The carriage trade was ready to exchange their heavy foreign cars for the easy handling American lightweight designs. An editorial of 1905 stressed the notion that the long wheel base of foreign cars was a great nuisance, brought on by the fad of side doors, and underscored the point that "doors are an imported evil, doubtless suited to the aristocrats of Europe, but wholly un-American and unnecessary."

In 1906, ten years after the automobile had first made its appearance, the American Medical Association published a symposium on the use of this new vehicle by physicians. A Dr. Stinson of San Francisco reported spending $566 for four months repairs to his $983 one cylinder model. Out on the East Coast at Dorchester, Massachusetts, however, things went somewhat better; a Dr. Charles Sylvester found that his car upkeep for seven months totalled $159.65, while his horse upkeep for a comparable period totalled $268.10,—not including the money lost on horse races. The doctors conditionally endorsed the automobile, the first group ever to consider it as useful. Some makers promptly announced "doctors models".

American automobile companies now sprang up on every side. Literally hundreds of new makes were announced each year. This was because plenty of motor hobbyists in all parts of the country were willing to put up the few thousand dollars required to turn out a model, named perhaps after them or their fair city or even after their dog. The typical factory was a large shed serving as an assembly plant. To this was brought an engine from a gas engine factory, a transmission from a gear factory and a frame from a machine shop; then some individual brass and body work, an eye catching name, and the company set forth to sell its new product. Demand for cars far exceeded supply, so sales costs were negligible. Exhibiting the model at the annual New York Auto Show was all that was needed. Potential buyers, attracted by some individual gadget or detail, would put in a down payment, and with this the parts could be ordered and the assembly job started. What an array these individual creations made is indicated in some of the accompanying pictures. Their names were myriad, almost beyond recall.

First there were the products of the Association of Licensed Automobile Manufacturers, a group of the old line companies (except Ford) that paid George Seldon, a far better patent lawyer than an inventor, a royalty on every car made. Ford's hold-out was example enough to encourage every fly-by-night concern not to bother with the royalty issue. Numerous suits were started by Seldon and all unlicensed manufacturers, their dealers and car buyers were warned that they were liable to infringement. Undaunted, everybody went right ahead, many to fall by the wayside, not for patent infringement, but for plain failure to deliver the goods. Who today remembers the Heine-Telox of San Francisco, the Tourist of Los Angeles, the Twyford of Houston, the Touraine of Philadelphia and the Triumph of Chicago, to mention only a few T's. All were pretty poor cars. The Triumph, according to one owner, made anything but triumphal progress in a 12 hour trek across the Arizona desert. There were three punctures, each necessitating repair on the spot with inflation by means of a hand pump. There was a broken spring, poorly repaired by a wrapping of baling wire. The radiator sprang a leak and let out water almost as fast as it was poured in. In order to get the engine to negotiate the smallest knoll a passenger had to blow on the gas tank to provide enough pressure for gas to get to the engine. Finally, the car ran so sluggish, it had to be literally pushed into a wayside repair station.

Aside from the difficulties of shoestring financing, there were two major reasons why so very few car concerns of this period survived. One was that their product simply was not equal to the rigors of road travel in those days; the other was the lack of service facilities, for even the most rugged of

VACATION SUGGESTION

THE PACE THAT KILLS

automobiles requires some attention when on tour. Some manufacturers, instead of campaigning for better roads and organizing dealer servicing on a cross country basis, put all their faith in the mere power of words. A catchy advertising phrase would substitute for a dependable motor—"Searchmont applied to autos has the same significance as 'sterling' when applied to silver. It denotes the best." "The Dumont flies but never falters." "The Union climbs hills as quietly as a high-grade sewing machine." "The full grown Flint, with her eighteen coats of paint and everything to match including a muffler that muffles." "The Reliable Dayton . . . first real successor to the horse . . . same road clearance as a carriage, and maintained at less cost per mile." Some of the slogans had a way of backfiring, as many an irate owner who acquired a mechanical liability was quick to point out.

"Why not the Glide, it's the best way to go."

"Catercar,—the car ahead, no gears to strip, just a gentle push."

"Baldner is the only car on the market that coasts."

"Corbin, the car of destiny, the repairman's dream."

"The Remington is built without complications . . . no expense necessary to lay it up for the winter."

"A Rig that runs . . . you can take out the transmission gears without removing the seat."

"Cleveland cars come back oftener than most . . . the auto for women."

"The Grout steamcar starts with a match and runs one hundred miles without stopping."

"The Moon motor motes . . . absolutely noiseless."

Even the fairly dependable cars of the period were given to extravagant claims. When Buick sent out an ad "Built to run and does it," a buyer notified the company that their punctuation was off—the statement should have read "Built to run, and does it?" When the Olds was said to be able to "negotiate any hill or travel any snow or mud you care to try," someone pointed out that few cared to try after one

How is she at hill climbing?

My dear sir, you'd never know you were on a hill if it wasn't for other cars blocking the way.

Slow up driver. Do you want to kill us both?

I'm new at this job, guv-'nor. I was just going to ask you which o' them things is the brake.

First Chauffeur: I get rattled when I see a woman cross the street in front of me.

The Second: Yes, so do I. They wear so many pins in their hats it's a sure puncture if you hit one.

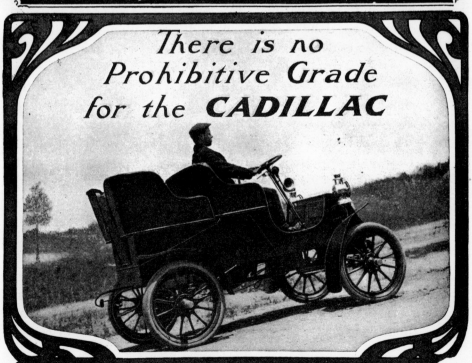

attempt. More time was usually spent tinkering in the home garage than running the car on the road.

The lack of servicing facilities would be nothing short of appalling to today's motorist. Drivers were expected to make any and all repairs from a punctured tire to a broken spring and went prepared to do so. A big tool kit and a goodly supply of spare parts always went with the new car. As if to distract the purchaser from the certain realities of roadside repairs, the dependability of the auto in contrast with the horse was stressed. "No accidents with the Oldsmobile," promised one dealer. "Car driving eliminates the danger of the horse's uncertain temper, sudden fright and unruly disposition . . . No runaways, a child can play with it with perfect safety. . . . And look at the fine body—new curved dash—no more criticism at having lost the horse." But not even Olds, the most popular car of the day and the most widely distributed, had anything like a satisfactory servicing organization. Most of its dealers had no garage facilities, so one took his chances with whatever wayside mechanic or blacksmith he might find. It is reliably reported that as much damage was done to early cars by the self-appointed tinkerers of the wayside as was caused by the hazards of the road.

Uncertain service and precarious roadbeds could not hold down the travel fever. The country was ready for the automobile even though not fully aware of the fact, ready to travel in something fast and snappy looking. Over ten million bicyclists took to the roads in 1900 for pleasure and picnicking They were organized into clubs in almost every town, and it was these organizations—more than the motor makers—who first put pressure on legislative bodies for better roads and streets. The bicycle had opened the way to low cost transportation and pleasure at the very time when the wealthy had fallen in love with the new self-propelled toy on wheels. As soon as motor manufacturers began to turn out gas buggies for a few hundred dollars, rich and poor alike set up a clamor for better roads. The power behind millions of votes began to have its effect. Almost overnight, states began to organize

FOUR BUICK BOMBSHELLS

$925.

18 H.P., Four Cylinders, Shaft Drive, Rumble Seat, Two Brakes, 5 Lamps and Generator, Michelin Tires.

This price is based on a coming output of 18,000 runabouts per annum. There are no other concerns in the country that can hope to duplicate the proposition without "going broke" trying it. It has taken the Buick Motor Co. two years and an expenditure of over $1,000,000 to get ready to turn these out at this price. It will take anyone else that tries it just as long. There can be no competition on this runabout before 1910. There is no Runabout on the market selling at under $1500 that can be compared with ours. Look them all over. **WE'LL LEAVE IT TO YOU.**

Model 10.

$1,275.

The same old reliable **22 H.P.,** two-cylinder car with new additions including 4 inch Michelin Tires, Full Eliptic Springs, longer Wheel Base, Straight Line Body, Spark and Throttle on top of Steering Wheel. Complete with 5 Lamps and Generator.

Model G same specification as above in Runabout Type, $1,175.

Model F.

$1,785.

Four-cylinder Touring Car or Roadster.

Complete equipment, Michelin tires.

30 H. P., unit power plant, 39-plate multiple disc clutch, sliding gear transmission, shaft drive, single rumble.

Magneto, $200 extra.
Double rumble, $50 extra.

Model S.

$2,550.

Four cylinders, cast in Pairs, **40 H. P.,** shaft drive, selective type gear change, long wheel base, complete with 5 Lamps, Michelin tires and Magneto.

As good as the "Big Fellows" for half the cost.

Model 5.

highway departments to pull themselves out of the mud and to give their citizens a chance to "open it up," "let her rip" and "step on the gas." Sparked by the rich, the twentieth century motor car was launched on the roads of America in a burst of uncertain speed.

The typical car of the 1905 epoch was an amusing creation, to say the least. It had progressed from the buggy seat box of the previous decade to include room for upwards of four people. The first innovation after the curved dash and rounded body design, was the inclusion of rear seats. How many have memories long enough to recall the rear entrance tonneau. It was perched over the back wheels like a tin basket. Occupants, usually women sat on jump seats facing each other, one hand on their heavy headgear, the other grasping a seat handle. Some times the chuck holes and thank-you-ma'ams of the road proved too much for these rear occupants and they were pitched out bodily. One such unfortunate lady sued her husband for divorce, claiming he abandoned her on the highway miles from home. The judge ruled against willful intent on the grounds that the machine made so much noise one could not expect the driver to know he had lost his wife en route. No such chance of escape was offered to the occupants of the early Grout car. They sat on jump seats in front of the driver "serving to protect him from the dust and obstacles of the road." If one can imagine himself sitting on the front bumper of a car in today's traffic, he may catch something of the feel of the early human windshield rider.

Neither front or rear jump seats were to last long in motor car design. In spite of cries by Duryea, Haynes and other early inventors, the longer wheel base and touring body with side doors came into widespread popularity. Winton and Rambler were among the first cars to move their power plant from the rear to the front for better distribution of weight and for more leg room for rear-seat occupants. There was still no protection from the weather, except for the fringed surrey tops and primitive glass fronts. People seemed to want the thrill of riding in the breeze. They went equipped with voluminous dusters, veils, leather coats and hot water bottles to protect themselves from exposure to the elements. The one man top and side curtains were yet to come.

The one strong cry in this era in which the automobile first captured the heart of America was "Speed with Roadability." Only those cars forged ahead that proved their endurance and ease of servicing. Consider the **Franklin, it** early earned an accolade as "The Doctor's car" due to its training of dealer servicemen. Or take the Cadillac which put out a catolog of parts and showed people how these could be installed as replacements. Recall that **Packard and Pierce** Arrow, built as quality cars from the very first, soon challenged the vogue for foreign cars among the wealthy, largely because they could be more readily serviced and repaired by American mechanics. Where quality cars went, the moderate priced ones had to follow suit and give the public something more than a shiny paint job with a lot of brass work to polish. A car had to run on the road as well as look classy in the showroom window.

Cartoon and comment of the period indicates a steady increase in problems connected with the automobile. When a worried chauffeur informed the owner that their car was out of control, he was ordered to "head for something inexpensive" to stop it. Another wealthy owner found the local blacksmith was the only man strong enough to crank his car and hired him to ride around and crank it. Accidental discovery of a spring valve to reduce the compression made cranking easy for the owner, and the blacksmith lost his job.

The following rules were humorously suggested in "Fleet Flashes of 1908." "1. On discovering an approaching team, the automobilist must stop offside and cover his machine with a tarpaulin painted to correspond with the scenery. 2. In case a horse will not pass an automobile, notwithstanding said tarpaulin, the automobilist will take his machine apart as rapidly as possible and conceal the parts in the grass. 3. Automobiles must be seasonably painted; that is, they

62

His Wife - It's the first time I've enjoyed this thing since you got it.

Stop John, There's a chicken on my lap!

Quick Nellie, snap the picture, here come the car's real owners.

I AM RESOLVED

Model 26-C. Chelsea, Removable Coupe Top, $1,600.00

I am resolved that I will not allow my business to crowd all the joyousness out of my life during the coming year.

I am resolved that I shall give myself and my family all the happiness I can, even if it costs me a little money to do it.

I am resolved that I shall get out into the sunshine; fill my lungs with fresh air; and let both the air and the sunshine filter through my whole being.

I am resolved that I shall eschew street cars and that my journeys to and from my business shall be made a source of health and pleasure instead of an annoyance and an exasperation.

In order to bring about this change in my manner of living I am resolved that I shall buy a

POPE Waverley ELECTRIC

must merge with the ensemble and not be startling. They must be green in the spring, golden in the summer, red in the autumn and white in the winter. 4. Automobilists running on country roads at night must send up a red rocket every mile and wait ten minutes for the road to clear. They may then proceed carefully, blowing their horns and shooting Roman candles.''

McClure's magazine reported the new industry of training auto drivers in the following fashion, ''a special instructor's cab is used by the Lightning Learning Company. It has a flaring front platform with a solid wooden bumper, so it may crash into a stone curb or run down a lamppost without injury. The instructor takes his seat beside the learner, where he is provided with a special arrangement for cutting off the power and applying the brakes, should the vehicle escape the learner's control. . . . It takes at least a week to train a man so he can manage everything with perfect presence of mind.''

As for women riders, a doctor of the period reported— with a straight face— that... ''a speed of 20 miles an hour causes them acute mental suffering, nervous excitement, and circulatory disturbances. While on the road, such patients sit with tense muscles, rarely relaxing... They are constantly on the lookout for trouble . . . each approaching car, each curve in the road, each grade crossing is nothing short of mental agony. ''

Encounters with the law continually turned up new problems. In California, a man was arrested and fined for driving after dark as late as 1905. The constable making the arrest fired several shots into the tires before it stopped. But the irate motorist appealed his case to the state supreme court and won for himself and other nighthawks the right to travel the highways after dark.

In another court action, this time lost, the Police Commissioners of New York City were enjoined to issue badges to chauffeurs, so that the latter might arrest people who hurled rocks and vegetables at them from the street. . . . And the officials of the Brooklyn Ferry ordered that autos could not be stopped and pushed on and off the Ferry by man; a team of horses had to be hitched to the gas buggy before it could be taken aboard.

Although the auto had captured high class fancy, the horse was still king of the highway, so far as custom decreed. Drivers of horse drawn vehicles could act as rude as they pleased, whereas the owner of an upstart auto had to be a model of politeness. The situation was memorialized in a popular postcard, showing a farmer letting his horse rest in the middle of the road, with a puffing automobile at his rear . . . the caption—toot and be durned. Out in Cohocton, Ohio, a woman in a farm wagon brought an approaching automobile to a stop by threatening the party of motorists with her rawhide whip.

That early touring was great sport after all is evidenced by reminiscences of the period. Bellamy Partridge, author of "Excuse My Dust," recalls that with a party of four he made a "Little Journey" to the home of Elbert Hubbard and his Roycrafters at East Aurora, N. Y. "In our soul-searing grind of 112 miles," he says, "we had the usual number of punctures; but on only one occasion was I compelled to put into a blacksmith shop for repairs. The village smith was willing enough to make the repairs, but he was very careful not to get too near the supply of gasoline for fear the smell might frighten the horses that were brought in for shoeing . . . ."

Another early touring addict recalls that most people preferred to tour New England because of the then so called excellence of their roads. Transcontinental treks were practically out of the question, and one who tried it found not a single filling station from New York to San Francisco in 1910.

The memoirs of Alfred P. Sloan, Jr., carry this account of his first car. "There was no windshield, no top and nothing more than absolutely necessary. Under the back seat, however, was a spare magneto, while bolted to the underside of the running boards were extra springs. The rest of the space

66

Lady Driver: Can you show us the way to Great Missden, please?
Weary Willie: Certainly, Miss. 'op up Joe. Anything to oblige a lady.

Automobilist: My friend, can you show me the way to Speedville?
Pedestrian: Why, yes sir; I'm going that way myself; just follow me.

"Mobile" Rapid Transit Route through Wall Street

**RUNNING FROM WALL STREET FERRY AND HANOVER SQUARE THROUGH
WALL STREET TO RECTOR TO NEW JERSEY CENTRAL FERRY,
WITH TERMINAL AT PENNSYLVANIA RAILWAY FERRY.**

*The "Mobile" Company of America has been the first either in Europe or
America to produce a practicable Wagonette, solving the problem of rapid transit.*

*They can be operated at from fifteen to twenty miles per hour or at any
rate of speed to suit the most crowded street.*

*To tear up Wall Street and provide a street-car plant to the route now be-
ing covered by the "Mobile" Rapid Transit Wagonettes would cost from half to
a million dollars. Three Wagonettes costing but $4,800 will give a service of
one wagon every five minutes.*

was taken up with spare tires and a Prestolite air tank. You lit the headlights with a match.''

But the cream of all reminiscences comes from an old time motor addict from the State of Maine, who writes:

''Imagine yourself, back in the year 1 9 0 5, stalled in an isolated community. Inquiry reveals that an 'expert' auto mechanic is located about 10 miles away. You contact this repair-man via the 'party-line', and finally the expert arrives, duly attired in cap, goggles, leather coat, gauntlet gloves and leather leggings, and driving a gothic-boned horse in an ancient buggy. While your glazed eyes digest this ensemble in conjunction with such lowly means of locomotion, your repair-man unlimbers a meek little bicycle repair-kit, a monkey-wrench and a carpenter's hammer and sets to work. When he begins to draw on the local black-smith shop for supplemental tools, you begin to feel that the engagement is going to be a serious mistake. But of course it is too late to say anything. Only then subsequent conversation reveals the awful fact that the 'expert' is one of a crop of rural graduates from an automobile correspondence school, and your car is the guinea pig for his first actual experience. So you interfere, gathering up the pieces of your disembowelled engine, and ship the whole car to the nearest agency—by freight.''

What were the really good cars of the period. ''The Reo, Rambler, Buick and Packard were very good,'' recalls the Maine Old Timer. ''Practically all the others were enough to make their owners curse God and long to die.''

All cars, good and poor alike, joined their owners in the battle for the roads. This battle was led by three hardy souls, Roy Chapin, an early associate in the manufacture of the little Oldsmobile, Harvey Firestone, the tire manufacturer and Charles G. Glidden, a millionaire hobby addict of the new machine. At the time Chapin helped launch the United States Office of Public Roads in 1904, less than 200,000 out of a total of more than 2,000,000 miles of rural roads in the country were even surfaced with gravel. Farmers did most of the road work, working out their taxes by dragging a stone boat

The spirit of the age—"Give her a little more gas, Nurse!"

"Please mister, give my sister a ride. She's got the bug bad."

JUDGE cartoons (by Peters and Conacher) mark a new generation's interest.

over the road to smooth out the ruts and fill in the chuck holes. Under Chapin and Firestone, states began to compete with each other for good roads improvement, and the Lincoln Highway, our first national transcontinental route, was launched.

Finally, there was Charles G. Glidden and his tours. This wealthy New England industrialist had taken a fortune out of his business which he used to indulge his new found hobby of automobiling. He won the American Automobile Association's cross-country tour from New York City to the Louisiana Purchase Exposition in St. Louis. Spurred on by this "truly epic flight," the A. A. A. began in 1905 the sponsoring of yearly cross-country "Reliability Tours" to sell the public on the practicality of the automobile and the need to provide it with the proper highways. The tours were named in honor of Glidden, who put up the trophies for the winners. From 1905 to 1911, when their place was taken by the newly organized Indianapolis 500 mile race classic, the Glidden tour victory was the greatest prize an automobile manufacturer could win for his car. The events were highly competitive affairs. They were charted over mountains and rough roads, East and West, North and South. All cars entered traveled as a pack, preceded by all the fanfare of advance publicity that America is famous for.

Rules for the Tour included strict time schedules for departure and arrival at morning, noon and night control points. Penalties were invoked for stoppages or repairs caused by mechanical or tire troubles; replacement of parts carried heavy penalties on the scoring system. To prevent night work on contestants' automobiles, hoods were locked down by Tour officials.

Millions of people witnessed these contests from 1904 to their end in 1913. They furnished the highlights of comedy and tragedy, publicity and experience, through the most vital years in the development of automobiles and good roads. The first run was a course of approximately 1,000 meandering miles from New York to Bretton Woods, New Hampshire. Of

60 H. P., $4,000.
F. O. B. Factory.

The Thomas - Flyer.

THE reliability of the 60 H. P. Thomas has at once been demonstrated and developed by two vitally important factors.

The use of the car in the hands of more than a thousand owners has proven its reliability; and the invaluable information gained by this experience has perfected that reliability.

Again, the wonderful victories won last year vindicated the absolute trustworthiness of Thomas construction — and helped us to make it still more trustworthy.

World's records, long-distance trials, and endurance contests—by winning every event of note in which it was entered the Thomas proved itself the greatest car of 1906 and paved the way for a greater car in 1907.

Years of exhaustive experience devoted exclusively to building high-powered cars; a corps of the most eminent engineers in Europe engaged with our own splendid mechanical force; and four of the most perfectly equipped factories in the world — is it surprising that a thousand owners testify to its unvarying reliability?

Last year the 60 H. P. Thomas literally stampeded the market. This year, with vastly increased facilities, history is repeating itself. We are perfectly disinterested in advising you to confer as soon as possible with your Thomas representative.

E. R. THOMAS COMPANY, Buffalo, N. Y.

Members Association Licensed Automobile Manufacturers.

KNOX

Thirty Horse-Power

on the road is better than fifty in the catalogue.
It is on the road you need it, and where, in the
Model "H"

KNOX WATERLESS

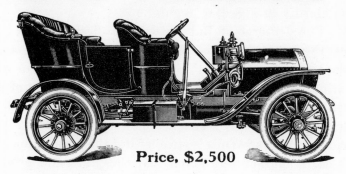

Price, $2,500

you get it. It is why the "H" has outrun and
outclimbed every other car of its class.

KNOX quality— standard for seven years—guarantees
its wearability. Weight, 2,250 pounds, actual; 102-inch
wheel-base; 32 x 4-inch tires; three-speed selective transmission; positive automatic oiling; compensating car-
buretter; dead-stop brakes; direct cooling; three-point
suspension; straight shaft drive; long, easy springs; speed
from 4 to 40 miles an hour.

*Write for illustrated catalogue and technical descrip-
tion; they are text-books on automobile construction.*

KNOX AUTOMOBILE COMPANY

Member Association Licensed Automobile Manufacturers
SPRINGFIELD, MASS.

the thirty-three cars entered, fully half were soon bogged
down in mud to the axles. Farmers along the route reaped a
handy profit by hauling the unfortunates to the nearest town
for repairs, and when the rustics could not profit in this manner, they strung ropes across the road to stop the speedsters.
Many a Glidden tourist barely escaped being beheaded, as
brakes were none too good in those days. If the rural Justices
could not fine a motorist for speeding, he could always be
hauled up for obstructing the road or frightening horses. The
development of the automobile had outstripped the law, and
it was some years before the motorist was to have some protection from this sort of thing. The tour officials did what
they could to stop gouging; they urged Tourists to carry their
own shovels and planks and to develop self reliance. Also
they tried to get local authorities to permit a maximum speed
of ten miles an hour through their town—the first attempt at
standardizing speeding regulations.

Percy Pierce of Buffalo won the first Glidden tour with
his Pierce Arrow, and the second tour starting from that
place was also won by Pierce. This was the tour in which the
various steam cars literally burned themselves out of the competitive picture, so far as auto sales were concerned. On the
first day Webb Jay's steamer blew up and burned. The second day Walter White's steamer did the same thing. As soon
as car manufacturers noted that the jokes and grief of contestants was getting more publicity than the performance of
the good cars, their interest in the Glidden tours began to
wane. Yet this had its place in eliminating cars that could
not make the grade mechanically. As for the adverse publicity given the poor roads of some sections and states, that
was even more beneficial in bringing about improvement.

Popular interest in the mishaps of the Glidden tours
began to abate about the time that mishaps were no longer
of interest. The Tour—and related developments—had served
its purpose well. Out of what was first a crude experimental
production, the automobile now emerged as an accepted factor
in American Life. It was still more a rich man's fancy than

Excuse my dust!

Their fallen foe!

Oh, if you were only a horse!

a possession for every man. Its owners were considered to be either millionaires or damned fools. If you owned a car in those days it meant that about thirty per cent would be added to all your other bills. The theory was that anyone who could afford to own a car could afford to pay a stiff price for everything else—and was a sucker to boot. Pioneer owners were imposed on by repairmen to a point that would make Al Capone and Captain Kidd look like philanthropists. Drivers in the Glidden tours were referred to as "aristocrats" and grocery stores along the way held them up with suddenly rocketed prices for gasoline. Hotels trippled their rates. Girls hung around hoping to catch the eye of some promising young "millionaire."

The funny part about this was that many early car owners were not rich men at all. A scandalous number of people mortgaged their homes to purchase a car. For the automobile was the new symbol of eclat . . . the thing that one must have to keep in the social whirl. It was no longer looked upon with derision and scorn, but with longing and envy. And the dream of a car in every garage was yet only a dream. Henry Ford had scarcely been heard from.

In 1907 Town & Country published this fashion photograph, captioned "Ready for the Christmas Motor Trip". It was additionally subtitled "The manner in which motorists are attired to withstand the severest winter weather."

Can you identify them? Insert the proper numbers. 1903 Studebaker........,
1903 Rambler, ...,   1904 Searchmont........,   1902 Columbia........,   1903
Haynes.........

Can you identify them? 1906 Winton, $2500........, 1907 De Luxe, $4750........, 1906 Northern, $1800.........

1

2

3

Can you identify them? 1906 Elmore, $2500........,   1904 Wayne, $2500........,
1908 Stevens Duryea, $2900.........

Can you identify them?   1907 Deere, $2500........,   1907 Thomas, $4000........,
1907 Autocar, $3000.........

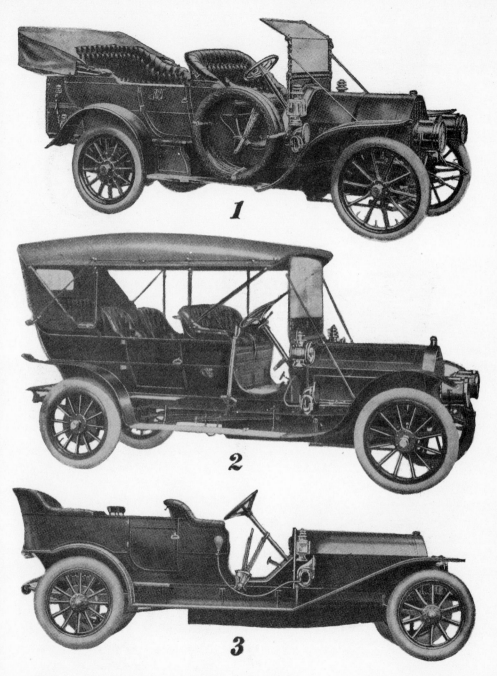

Can you identify them? 1907 Pope Toledo, $3500........,   1908 Pierce Arrow, $5500........,   1909 Premier, $3500........

Can you identify them? 1907 Marmon, $2500........,   1907 National, $3500
........,   1907 Columbia, $4500........

Can you identify them? 1905 Locomobile, $2800........, 1907 Cadillac, $2000
........, 1908 Reo, $1250......... All cars are listed in order shown top to bottom.

CHAPTER III

19

15

Poor Man's Lizzy....

THE year 1915 saw the automobile launched on a new scale. Brass had given way to black enamel, the left hand drive replaced the right, and the electric starter was being put on the more expensive cars. In the luxury class it was still anybody's market. But the cheap car field belonged to one man, and his name was Ford. People who had never dreamed of owning an auto a few years back now found themselves in possession of dependable low cost transportation,—the Model T.

Until Henry Ford produced the Model T, one had to be pretty well-off to own a car. The cars of the 1905 era were costing from $2,000 to $3,000 or even more,—way out of the reach of the average American family. Two-thirds of the 90,000,000 population were farmers and the average cash income at this time was under $500.00 a year. The first Model T wasn't a cheap car either. It cost $850.00 F. O. B. Detroit. But by 1913 Ford had the price down to $550.00, by 1915 it was down to $365.00, and the joke went, "one day—one dollar, one year—one Ford."

The Model T looked for all the world like a black tin bathtub mounted on four wheels. It had a little box covering the motor, and in front of that was the crank that either started the car or broke an arm. The gas tank was located under the seat, an arrangement necessitating that all dismount for each refueling. Its planetary transmission and magneto spark made operation a thing out of this world. To get under way, the spark lever first had to be adjusted, being

HOME FROM HARVARD

Harrison Cady (Life '10) shows why the auto is approved by the "old man."

careful not to get a huge jolt of electricity down the arm. Then one cranked, leaped over the imitation door into the driver's seat and pushed up the gas lever to a point where the whole machine seemed about to burst apart, finally stepped on the left "clutch" pedal. This was followed by much grinding and groaning of "low" as the Model T quivered and shook itself into motion. Once the car was rolling, another pedal was used to jerk the machine into "high."

In its heyday the Model T wore three-inch clincher tires, held under 60 pounds of air pressure. Punctures were frequent, so a spare casing or two was carried as regular equipment plus an even larger number of inner tubes. One made the repairs on the road, or if tired of this, wrapped ropes around the wheels. Not until its latter days did the Model T adopt demountable rims, a generator, battery, and such accessories as a speedometer. Wags insisted this caused a coo-coo bird to sing "Nearer my God to Thee" whenever the speed got up to 40 miles an hour.

The first truly universal car rode into popularity with the help of widespread service facilities and standardized parts. It did not happen overnight. During the first decade of the century, few dealers made any attempt to repair the make of car they sold. If they did send for a replacement part from the factory, chances were that this would not fit when received,—or the order might be altogether ignored. Early car owners had no conception of the modern garage, devoted almost exclusively to servicing one make of car. They favored buying big expensive models as the best way of avoiding road troubles. Besides, many were wealthy enough to employ a private chauffeur—mechanic to keep their machine in running order. Other owners were of sufficient mechanical bent themselves that, with the help of an occasional blacksmith, they serviced their own needs. Less fortunate souls—forced to rely upon the uncertain skills and practices of roadside tinkerers—left the new cars alone.

The combination of a good cheap car with a policy that really serviced was what turned the trick for Henry Ford,

"Why don't you get someone else to crank it, John? We can't sit here forever.

"I'll give you just five more minutes to get it running. Else we're taking the last street car home."

"You experience the thank-you-ma'm"; Thus did Strothmann illustrate pleasures of desert travel.

The famed W. Herndon Oldsmobile poster of 1910 showed car beating a train.

Two famous cartoons from 1910 Judge

Above: Getting Ready for the Sunday Push, by Tousay.
Below: Puzzle Picture. What is the gentleman going to buy?

and put his 'Tin Lizzy,' potentially at least, within reach of every man. Though widely credited with 'creating' this devolopment, it was actually a series of lucky breaks rather than inspired revelation that put across the so-called ''Ford idea.''

Looking backwards, it seems that Ford captured the most aggressive, reliable and conscientious dealers in most communities simply because he happened to be in a position **to supply interchangeable parts more rapidly than other manufacturers. All** buyers in the early days paid cash for their cars, and the get-rich-quick dealer had no interest in a model beyond getting it delivered. Materials were poor, roads still terrific, breakdowns frequent. Irate owners came back on the dealer for help when the machine failed to run. This was bad local publicity. It hurt sales. So if a dealer was at all interested in surviving in a community, he was almost forced to do something about servicing the cars he sold. It did not take people in the home town long to find that John Smith stood behind the cars he sold and would see that they were kept running. After 1910, when the idea of motor transportation was generally accepted as the coming thing, smart buyers tended to pick dealers rather than car names. ''I understand John Smith is handling the Studebaker this year,'' said one. ''Well, that's enough for me,'' was the typical reply, ''Any car that John handles you can depend upon to make good—or else.'' Ford's trick—or lucky break—lay in capturing enough John Smith's to build the finest home front sales force in the country. He did it by supplying workable replacement parts where other car manufacturers were indifferent and failed.

Consider the plight of conscientious dealers who looked to the manufacturer for help in keeping their cars running. Sometimes their most frantic calls on the factory for help on parts were not even answered. At best, the factory service was slow, desultory, and the rough castings of parts had to be machined when received. The dealer's reaction to all this can be imagined. If he could not get cooperation from one

92

factory, he tended to shift his allegiance to a new agency.
Now Henry Ford was one of the first to realize the necessity
of providing service, so that demand and confidence in his
cars would be maintained. Very early, therefore, he began to
select as dealers, men who could be depended upon to service
the cars they sold and to cooperate with their every need.
The situation also worked in reverse, for with Ford interested in service parts, service conscious dealers turned to him.
By 1910 everyone was convinced that the automobile was
potentially more economical than the horse, (At least, it did
not eat hay when not in use.) The one seeming drawback was
the lack of easy repairs to "keep 'em running." Other things
equal, that car would win most widespread acceptance that
would first offer easy, economical repair service on a country-
wide basis. And Ford was ready for this.

Back in 1905, when he was still making his expensive
model K cars, Ford was interested in providing parts to
keep them running. His factory only an assembly plant for
parts made elsewhere, he worked for standardization and
precision milling so that he could take an item off the stock-
pile and have it fit into either a new assembly or a repair job.
His dealers were encouraged to keep their customers happy—
and incidentally to win new ones—by telegraphing the Ford
plant for replacements. Ford supplied everything to the best
of his ability, carefully noting what parts most frequently
broke and wore out. As soon as demand became sufficient
to make it worthwhile, the company began to manufacture
the parts themselves and to supply their dealers with an
assortment of replacement parts in advance of breakdown.
Think what this meant to the harried motorist, whose car
had broken down enroute to a family reunion or some other
event. If he could pull into a convenient garage and get matters fixed up within an hour or so, you can be sure he was certain that he had the best car on the road, no matter how it
compared in looks or speed or price with the rest of the field.

As a car, Ford's new low-cost Model T was not an instan-
taneous hit. It had less class than the Olds, cost more than

"Henry! You're driving up on the sidewalk!"

Such startled comments were frequently heard in Pittsburgh, Pennsylvania in December, 1913, when here was opened the first "drive in" service station in the world. It was the first sign of a new attitude toward the motorist that was to put his convenience first

This development was pioneered by

GULF REFINING COMPANY

Until the 1920's most motorists bought their gasoline from a hand pump in front of the local hardware store. Gas was frequently dirty and had to be strained before being poured into the automobile's gas tank. Pioneer service stations sprang up in Pennsylvania, where gas was first discovered. From that early beginning (typified in the period advertisement above), grew a three-billion dollar industry. This early service station is a far cry from today's gaseterias, where motorists drive up to the pump, fill their own tanks and deposit payment in a slot.

the model introduced by Sears Roebuck and Company, and had the planetary type of clutch-transmission box that was already going out of date. But by 1910 its fine service record was apparent and Model T was well launched toward universal popularity, and by 1915—the middle of our decade—it had arrived.

This could be called the era of the Common-man, so far as cars went. Expensive creations were made and as widely sold as ever. Doctors, always in the forefront in the utility use of cars, were buying models of all descriptions and taking them to their calls over all kinds of roads; but, under Ford's leadership, it became popular to own a popular-priced automobile. Taken out of the luxury class, more and more people began to speak of it as a "necessity."

A rash of new jokes and new songs broke over the land. The Ford was represented in picture and word as a personified object, temperamental, bumptious, but all in all dependable. The jokes made as much of mankind's inevitable need for it as upon the caprices of the car itself. All this Ford encouraged as the best of free advertising. He is even rumored to have backed publication of Adam Allen's famed book, "The Tin Lizzy."

Ford's ability to undersell all competition for like quality stemmed from the fact that one of his earliest associates, Walter Flanders, was a genius of production efficiency. No sooner was this man installed as factory superintendent than he rearranged machinery so that manufacture was stepped up from 20 to 150 cars a day. This was more than the infant Ford organization could sell. Looking into matters from the sales end, Flanders decided that the machine still looked more like a buggy than an automobile. By 1910 he had the Model T dressed up in full fenders and running boards, the idea sold to Ford, and demand exceeding supply.

This Walter Flanders was a fabulous creature who fought the battle of mass production by day and had energy still to burn with wine, women and song at night. The circumspect Henry Ford disapproved of Flanders' social life, the

96

Early automotive assembly line—an American achievement.

same as he did that of the rough and ready Dodge Brothers who made his motors. But, as usual, he compromised his personal feelings to give competence its due. Only once did he let his private tastes influence his business judgement.

The story is told that Charles Statdorf, whose magneto coil was sparking the 1912 Ford, invited Henry, Flanders and some other auto bigwigs to a private supper party after the New York automobile show. When the guests arrived, some were surprised to find twice as many covers laid as there were men at the party. The arrangement was promptly explained by the arrival of a bevy of young women in revealing evening gowns. They took the empty chairs and indicated without much encouragement a willingness to move to the lap of the man on their right. Splitdorf and Flanders welcomed this diversion. Ford did not. He went straightway to the hotel lobby, where he encountered by chance another magneto manufacturer, Heinz. . . . People wondered the next year why Ford had adopted a new magneto contraption; but the real reason for the change was never given out.

Regardless of how it was sparked, the Model T moved onward and upward in public demand. Around ten thousand were sold yearly at the beginning of the decade, around a million a year when it closed. Over fifteen million Fords were made and sold to Mr. America before the Model T lost out in popular fancy. Ford made himself many times a millionaire, paid his workers the unheard of wage of $5.00 a day, was boomed for President of the United States.

Flushed with success, Ford could be as arbitrary as he pleased. He refused to pay royalties on the Seldon patent—unlike most other important car manufacturers of the day, and eventually broke the Seldon case in the Supreme Court. He also refused to add many of the improvements of the decade to the Model T,—transmission gears, a lower chassis for greater ease in riding, above all the self-starter, generator and electric storage battery. He refused to 'style' his car. "Any customer," he said, "can have a 'Ford painted any color as long as it is black." And the public, in general,

Ford produced the Model T in 1908

EVOLUTION OF THE FORD. The early model was a two cylinder, chain drive, rear entrance affair costing over $1,000. Next came the Model T costing around $600. In its final state (top of page) Model T was priced at $365, giving rise to a nation-wide gag: "One day, one dollar; one year, one Ford."

$1 96

We offer here a woman's dust coat made of selected tan linen cut on approved lines, single breasted mannish effect, with tailored stitched seam down the center of the back; on each side of the front is a convenient patch pocket carefully finished with rows of machine stitching; the regulation coat sleeve is provided with a comfortable wind shield; the strong b o n e buttons effecting the closing b u t t o n through w e l l made buttonholes; sizes 34 to 44 inch bust measure; length 52 inches. Just the garment for general wear, walking, driving or motoring, and at the remarkably low p r i c e quoted you can afford to have a full supply for yourself and friend's use; similar coats are being selected daily by critical shoppers in the motoring department of our large department store.

82B12401 Single Breasted Dust Coat; special price each $1.96

$1 96

Serviceable long coat in single breasted mannish style of excellent quality heavy oxford grey chambray. Front and back out generously full, with convenient deep p a t c h pockets on either side of the front, a n d carefully stitched center seam down the back; the regulation coat sleeve is provided with inside wind shield; the entire garment is carefully tailored and finished throughout, and will be found especially desirable for general out-door wear; sizes 34 to 44 inch bust; length 52 inches. You can't afford to waste money by buying from other retail dealers when you can secure such excellent value as represented in this garment at unapproachable prices; remember you are at liberty to return any unsatisfactory purchase at any time.

82B12402 Single Breasted Dust Coat; special price each.................. $1.96

$2 74

Full length Coat of good quality natural tan linen, cut in severe mannish style, full front, single breasted, fastening with five large buttons; loose fitting back has carefully stitched center seam; regulation sleeve with fashionable inside wind shield, close fitting turn down collar; carefully finished of excellent wearing material, and a coat that will be much in demand all season for the many occasions requiring an outer garment of this character; 34 to 44 inch bust; length 52 inches, every detail in the construction of this garment has had as careful attention as that given to coats retailing at much higher prices; if you order one of these garments we feel sure you will be so pleased with it that you will be numbered among our thousands of satisfied mail order buyers.

82B12403 Single Breasted Dust Coat; special price each. $2.74

$2 96

Fashionable f u l l leng traveling c o a t made of he c o t t o n chambray semi-fit with full double breasted fr finished with close fitting c lar; the regulation coat slee finished with deep turned b cuff held together with t small buttons; l a r g e pa pockets have neatly stitc flaps; every requirement f general outdoor garment been met in this model, a the attractive price will ma it a desirable addition to y wardrobe; sizes 34 to 44 in bust; length 52 inches; in lecting this number you c feel assured that you are sec ing the best coat it is possi to produce for the money; shoddy or shop worn garme are handled by us at any pri satisfaction guaranteed alwa or your money will be refund

82B12404 Double Breast Dust Coat; special price each. $2.9

Apparel For the Motorist

For a man requiring one or [mor]e of these indispensable [dus]t coats at moderate price we [hav]e designed this serviceable [gar]ment made of natural tan [li]n, in double breasted effect, [but]toning close to the neck if [desi]red for added protection [aga]inst dust and dirt. The [to]p pockets are well finished; [the] bone buttons effecting the [clo]sing are good and strong to [with]stand general wear and [tea]r; the full fashioned sleeve [is f]itted with wind cuff; in fact [no] feature which would add to [the] serviceability of this gar[men]t has been overlooked; 52 [inc]hes long and in 34 to 44 [inc]h chest measure; note the [exc]eptionally low price we [quo]te, compare this garment [wi]th similar coats offered else[wh]ere at much higher prices, [and] save money by purchasing [you]r coats from us.
82B12501 Motor [Dust] Coat. Price each.. **$1.49**

Correctly cut motor dust coats, full roomy model 52 inches long, designed to button close to neck for added protection against dust and dirt, or may be worn open as shown in illustration; the well shaped sleeve has fashionable wind cuff, and the two deep slashed pockets are tailored stitched and well finished; coat made from good wearing quality tan khaki cloth, which is very popular for this style of a garment; four strong bone buttons and well made buttonholes fasten the coat down the front; you need not hesitate a minute about selecting this number because it will be found exactly as represented, a well made coat, of good serviceable material designed to meet the requirements of a general wear dust coat; sizes 34 to 44 chest.
82B12502 Motor Dust Coat. Price each.. **$1.96**

In this natural linene full loose model dust coat you will secure the best garment that can be produced for the money. The material has been selected for its service giving qualities. The single breasted front buttons with bone buttons through carefully finished buttonholes; the two piece collar can be fastened close about the neck if desired for protection against dust and dirt; a stitched belt of self material confines the fullness in the back; two outside patch pockets are carefully stitched and finished; wind cuffs in the full fashioned sleeves which are additionally trimmed with straps of self material; sizes 34 to 44 inch chest measure; length 52 inches; just the kind of a well tailored coat that you would expect to pay double the price we are asking at the ordinary retail stores.
82B12503 Motor Dust Coat. Price each.. **$2.96**

Dust Coat made from excellent quality dark grey mohair, which is universally popular for this class of garments. Designed in full loose double breasted model, with fullness belted in in the back and buttoning close to the neck with a well fitting collar; neat breast pocket, tailored stitched and furnished with a buttoned flap; the two deep slash pockets open through the coat which is a very great convenience in reaching the pockets of the inner clothing; full shaped sleeve with durable wind shield cuff trimmed with straps of self material; the large bone buttons button through carefully worked buttonholes; sizes 34 to 44 inch chest measure; length 52 inches; carefully finished throughout and exceptionally good value.
82B12504 Motor Dust Coat. Price each.. **$4.96**

AUTO SCARFS DRIVING

8F9561 $1.18

38F9578 78c

38F9558 $1.95

38F9570 69c

38F9551 59c

THIS SCARF is made of what is known as silk mull; however, it is only part silk. Hemstitched on both ends and comes in two lengths; about 25 inches wide, 90 inches long.

No. 38F9551	Light blue.	EACH
No. 38F9552	Pink.	
No. 38F9553	Champagne (Tan).	59c

Same scarf as above, but 55 inches long, and comes in the following colors:

No. 38F9575	Light blue.	EACH
No. 38F9576	Pink.	
No. 38F9577	Champagne (Tan).	39c

THE MOST WONDERFUL SCARF WE EVER HAD and the greatest value ever offered. Silk mull scarf, silk one way, with dots of the same colorings. Hemstitched on both ends. May be had in two lengths as quoted below, one a fair length, and the other very long. These scarfs come packed in fancy gift boxes. These numbers come 90 inches long and about 25 inches wide.

No. 38F9570	Cream-white.	
No. 38F9871	Champagne.	EACH
No. 38F9572	Black.	
No. 38F9560	Light blue.	69c

Sears Roebuck and Company takes a hand at popularizing the Turkish Scarf for Auto Wear. One must look diaphanous and demure despite dirt and dust.

stayed with him in all this. He made, by all odds, the best car on the market for its price. Aided and abetted by William Knudson, who took over production in 1913, Ford's assembly line methods drove prices down and down again. Farmers who had never dreamed of owning automobiles before, now could not afford to be without a Ford.

The experience of one Maine farmer, Chester Parker, is typical. "Before I got my Ford," he wrote his newspaper, "it took me a whole day to get my produce into town. Now I load the rear seat with butter, eggs and vegetables, seat myself on a fine soft cushion instead of a hard board covered with horse blankets, and away I go speeding without a jolt hard enough to crack one of my eggs. I can make the trip to town and back by noon, and besides saving a half-day's time, I get twenty percent better prices by being to market before the rest."

You can be sure that this owner thought of his Tin Lizzy with more affection than mirth. The Ford Joke landed in American folk-lore by the universal acceptability of the product despite its minor shortcomings. "Twist her Tail" and "Wind her Up," were the greetings exchanged over an old friend. Even owners who soon switched to expensive cars loaded with all the latest mechanical improvements will always remember Model T as their first car, the car that sold itself as a necessity of life.

Everybody who could get into the act shared the profits of selling low-priced cars to the mass market. Some Ford dealers retired as millionaires. Sears Roebuck and Company did a major business in selling Ford parts by mail. Companies were founded for the sole purpose of making improvements and accessories to dress up the Ford. Nor were other car manufacturers adverse to following where Ford led, notably the Maxwell, the Willys and the Chevrolet.

As sales of all cars mounted, the "automobile game" became the "automobile business." Wall Street became interested. There was capital available for expansion. A few makers, notably Ford, avoided banker control. Most of the

ACCESSORIES OF INTEREST TO MOTORIST

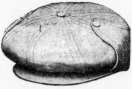

82B12801 Men's Motor-Cap, golf model, made of atural tan linen; unlined, finished with leather atband. Price 49c

82B12802 Men s Motoring cap of tan Khaki, unlined, finished with sweatband, special price each....... 49c

82B12803 Men's Motoring cap, two snap tourist model, made of natural tan linen, unlined, finished with price each........ 74c

82B12804 Men's Motoring cap, two snap tourist el of Dark Grey Mo lined. Special price each ....

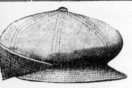

82B12806 Men's Motor-cap, Cracker Jack Mod-of natural tan linen with ched brim and visor un d. cial price each 98c

THE QUALITIES

Of our motoring Accessories e strictly first-class in every spect. In fact, the depart ent in our business devoted the sale of motoring wear g apparel and is the most tisfactory place in New ork City to purchase goods this character.

82B12807 Men's Motoring hat of Rubber; in Red, Black and tan to match Rubber shirt as described under No. 20. Special price each 69c

82B12808 Women's Motoring Cap with detachable silk hood to protect hair from dust in black, blue, grey and brown. Special price each $2.49

82B12809 Women hood, with mica front on over hat and ties abou of fine quality crepe de c blue, Alice blue, brown, tan and white. Special price

Allow 5c extra to pay postage if you want y of these goggles sent by mail.

82B12811 Rubber goggles n removable lens. A very good priced goggle. cial price each 47c

82B12814 Goggles, collapsible model in grey, tan and brown. Special price each 59c

82B12813 Goggles of tan leather four way model, patent hinge for lens. 64c

82B12812 Rubber gles, with removable le extra pair of smoked lens Special price each ....

Lined Gauntlet Glov

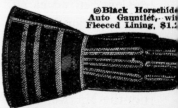

82B12816 Motoring Gauntlet Gloves Men. Medium size cuff in black or splendid quality, all regular s. cial price each $1.49

82B12817 Motoring Gauntlet gloves for Men, Exceptional value; black only: all regular sizes. Special price each 98c

◎**Black Horsehide Auto Gauntlet**, wit Fleeced Lining, $1.

W 20427◎—Men's lined auto gauntlet, ma medium weight oil tanned black horsehide Price, per pair ....◎

82B12818 Motoring Gauntlet Gloves Men, cut full, with large cuff in ck or tan; all regular sizes. cial price each $1.74

82B12819 Motoring Gauntlet Gloves for Men and Women; full size cuff in black or tan. Excellent value; all regular sizes. Special price each $1.96

◎**Lined Black Calfskin Automobile Gauntlet Glove, $2.50**◎

W 20435◎—Men's Automobile Gauntlet, of fine light weight calfskin leather; has ext flexible wrist and large 5½ inch deep leather

others—mechanics at heart—soon found themselves at the mercy of men who knew nothing of automobiles except that the public wanted to buy them. Towering over all in the financial wizardry of this decade was W. C. Durant. He put General Motors together, gave Ford his first real competition, brought millions of new capital into the industry and lost control of his colossus, all within ten short years.

It has been said that "the horse fell to Henry because Henry ate nothing while idle." No doubt such savings helped to put over the substitute. But neither the Ford nor any competing car of the 1910 decade can claim to have replaced the horse on a strictly economic issue. Social ferments quite apart from economics were gathering force. The tranquil note on which the century began had changed to the strident din of war. And while America was only dimly aware of the European holocaust, its slow-moving pattern of living was inevitably upset. . . . It was a restless age, with more and more people wanting to go more and more places faster than ever before. Cars took them on their way better than horses. They now serviced readily and repaired easily. Perfectly suited to the quickening tempo of the times, the automobile became a thing indivisible from those times.

Nowhere is the changing attitude of public acceptance more clearly evidenced than in the fiction cartoons and songs of the period. When the decade begun, the automobile was sufficiently new to inspire stories built around its novelty. Richard Harding Davis wrote the most famous, "The Scarlet Car," in which the auto itself was heroine; at the end of the decade the popular title was, "The Car Belongs To Mother."

In 1910, the Williamsons, C. and E. A., began their writing marathon,—book after book with the same basic plot. A poor little rich girl was advised to take a motor trip to Scotland or Timbuctoo as a possible way to restore health and vitality. Naturally, a stalwart young man has to go along to chauffeur the party over the almost impassable roads of the day. In the course of patching tires and cleaning spark-plugs, the young man falls violently in love with the heroine in the tonneau. After varying vicissitudes, girl joins boy in patching tires and cleaning spark-plugs. Health and appetite restored by such robust exercise, she proudly takes her place beside the erstwhile chauffeur, as much begrimed and happy they jolt back to home b a s e to be married.... Contrast such an unrealistic approach with the matter-of-fact story of later vintage, "Youth at the Wheel."

Early automobile stories had all the bad features of a tour de force. For mystery addicts there was Ellis' "The Phantom Auto." The problem novel is represented by "A Motor-Car Divorce." Children's books broke out in a rash of auto stories. Every famed juvenile character from the Rover Boys to Ruth Fielding went places in a car. Peck's Bad Boy, Tom Swift, The Campfire Girls and the Bobbsey Twins became involved with the new marvel. Personal exploits of motoring hardships had a wide sale, Street's "My Enemy, The Motor Car" and Teilheit's "Trouble Is My Master" being among the best. Poole lampooned a rich man's folly with "The Car of Croesus." Quite in contrast is the respectful "Book of Ford," the jolly "Poppy Ott and the Galloping Snail," the exciting "Motor Maniacs" report of 1918 racing.

Look now at the song cycle. When Bobby North and Al Jolson first rolled an automobile onto the stage and sang, "He had to get under, get out and get under," their audiences already knew by hearsay or experience that a motor trip was likely to end with the driver banging away under the car while his guests baked in the sun above. Their rendering of the later "Take Me Out For A Joy Ride" was keyed to an appreciation for swift, trouble-free motoring. People who sang the decade in with such numbers as "Society Craze," "The Benzine Buggy Man" and "The Gay Chauffeur," were seemingly convinced that the automobile was the toy of the wealthy. But they sang the decade out with ditties for every man, "Take A Little Ride With Me Baby," "When He Wanted To Love Her He Put Up The Cover" and "On The Back Seat of The Henry Ford."

THE FUTURE OF THE AUTOMOBILE: Early
cartoonists saw it as Extravagance Enthroned

WIPING OUT OLD SCORES

1910

THE HORSE IN 1951

1911

ONLY A DOG

1911

1913

"Come on, Billy, that ain't the kind we want anyway"

1913

THE SYMPATHETIC PEDESTRIAN

"IT MAY BE SLOW, BUT WE'LL GET HOME."

1906

"Just think, William! Probably the only pleasant break in the monotonous lives of these poor people is an occasional passer-by like curselves."

For nearly 54 years Life was a magazine of drawings, picturing the American scene. As a major U. S. phenomenon, the automobile came in for its fair share of Life's fun, satire, sentiment, and deadly serious crusade. Herewith a portfolio.

Reproduced courtesy Life and Time magazines.

B.C., 2500—CENTAUR

A.D., 1906—MOTAUR

1906

1908

IN 1918

THE RICH THEY RIDE IN AIRSHIPS, BUT THE POOR—

AUTOMOBILE NUMBER   1907

1906

1907

1908 (?)

Suppose we deliver a

Studebaker

Flanders "20"

Touring time is here; and you feel the urge of it.

Telephone the Studebaker dealer and have a "20" sent out tomorrow.

It will cost you $800—or $885, if it's fully equipped.

And what will you get—*will you get $800 worth ?*

Well, we don't know of a better $800 worth in the world.

We'd say that, even if you judged it only from the standpoint of size; and good looks; and workmanship; and material; and generous specifications.

But that isn't the main point.

The thing that ought to bring you to a decision to send for the "20" tomorrow is the certainty that you're not taking a chance.

It might be wise to take more time if the "20" were just *a* motor car.

But it's infinitely more than that —it's a *Studebaker* motor car.

Seventy-five thousand other owners have preceded you in the Studebaker 'testing out' process.

Sixty years of faithful performance have made the Studebaker word as good as gold.

Enormous productive capacity and world-wide distribution make the price right.

Yield to that impulse to get a car at once.

You're made absolutely safe by that name Studebaker.

Telephone the Studebaker dealer.

Take the children with you when you get the first demonstration tomorrow.

$800

It takes only a moment's reflection to see that mass interest and ownership of automobiles was creating new socio-economic problems. Registration and licensing of cars was at first very haphazard; but by 1910 most states had come around to charging a dollar or so, and giving the motorist a number that he could have painted on his car. Required liability insurance had scarcely been thought of. Driver's licenses were also far in the future. Anyone fron eight to eighty, who could get a motor car in motion was allowed on the highway. Crashes abounded. There were only two drivers in Kansas City around 1905 yet these somehow managed to meet one day in a head-on collision, which proves what could be accomplished with a bit of trying. There were also many clashes between motorists and the local constabulary. Animals and pedestrians hit in passing were proper game for a budding crop of ambulance chasers. The courts were filled with lawsuits seeking redress for property damage sustained when an unruly machine came to rest on someone's porch or favorite shade tree. One motorist turned the usual tables and sued a farmer for deliberately creating a sinkhole where the road passed his house, so that all cars would have to "Pay toll" by being hauled out.

The impact of general acceptance extended far beyond licensing problems and legal battles. One sociologist attributed the reduced birthrate to the fact that a young man, unable to afford both wife and automobile, too frequently chose the automobile. A doctor, however, suggested that the reduced birthrate was due to widespread miscarriages induced by riding in the jolting machines. An anthropologist insisted that the automobile would eventually improve the American breed, especially in sections where too much intermarriage was due to poor transportation facilities. He favored "extending the field of courtship" from the five mile radius of the horse and buggy to the fifty mile radius of the automobile. When educators and clergymen began to sound a warning about the dangers of the motor age, they were not thinking of property damage. Many a girl lost her virginity in an automobile. The business had taken on sociological as well as economic significance.

The shifting of people all over the United States during the World War had its effect on both manners and morals. Among other things, it started the American habit of "touring." Soldiers, released from training camps, wanted to show their new wives the sights they had seen while in uniform. A vacation by automobile became the aim of millions. Many who could ill afford it scraped money or credit together as down payment on a tin lizzy and had themselves a trip on gasoline begged, borrowed or stolen. Once acquired the motor car was never voluntarily relinquished by the masses. In one short decade, it had changed the pattern of American living.

All other developments, from Kettering's self starter to the Indianapolis Speedway and its "Knights of the Wheel" pale to insignificance as we "Watch the Ford's Go By." For not until Ford production, pricing and servicing entered the picture, snobbishness, social position and Veblen's "Conspicuous Consumption" lay behind ownership of a motor car. Purchasers were exhilarated by auto-intoxication—gave little thought of the practical uses of the invention.

But for Ford and other manufacturers quick recognition that their future rested in making automobiles for the mass and not for the class, the business would even today be on the same basis as is the building of motor boats and yachts—two pleasure devices still largely confined to the rich because of prohibitive costs.

Popularization of the automobile is a distinctly American achievement, brought about by American methods that standardized auto parts, created the assembly line and made for low cost and easy servicing. The Model T brought all these things. America loved its "Poor Man's Lizzy," built around it a derisive folklore which has now assumed the aura of nostalgic legend.

Official Program
Matinee
Automobile Races

Auspices of
Motor Dealers' Contest Association
of New York, Inc.

Brighton Beach Race Track
Monday, September 7th, 1914

When automobile dealers and manufacturers found the newspapers giving
main publicity to Glidden Tour breakdowns, they switched to sponsorship of
track races such as the one advertised above.

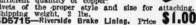

Sears Roebuck found it more profitable to sell parts for Fords than to market its own cars as shown by the catalog page above.

Electric Horn

$2⁴⁹

$2^{49}

This is an absolutely new horn. It gives a warning note that can be heard blocks away, and we are putting it on the market to meet a demand for a reliable horn of this character at a moderate cost. No pains have been spared to make this a first-class horn in every particular. The upkeep of this horn is merely nominal, being only ¼ ampere. Diameter of bell, 5 inches. Neat in appearance, finished in black enamel. Complete, with 12 feet of cable, attaching bulb and push button. Operates on any six-volt storage battery or five dry cells. Shipping weight, 6 pounds.

2K2798¾ Electric Short Horn. Enamel, black finish. Price, each **$2.49**

See the Auto Tire Sensation on Page 1020

Hand Mechanical Horn $3⁶⁸

A $5.00 Value

This fine horn has the Klaxon tone, and it does not require electricity to operate. Cam wheel is rotated by a train of carefully tooled gears instead of an electric motor. Gears develop high speed by merely pressing down push rod. This horn does not require expensive battery renewals or wiring. Emits powerful and far reaching warning. Bracket detachable and may be fastened to any flat surface or to top of door. Attractively finished in dull black.
2K2796 Hand Mechanical Horn, 6-inch nickeled bell. Size over all, 8½x8½ inches. Shpg. wt., 4 lbs. Price, each **$3.68**
2K2797 Hand Mechanical Horn, 4-inch bell. Size over all, 5½x5½ inches. Shipping weight, 3 pounds. Price, each **$3.38**

Klaxon Hand Actuated Horn

$7⁰⁰

This horn is another model of the hand actuated style. It works at any and at all times when needed, as it does not rely on bulb, wire, current or anything that is possible to get out of order. When you want a horn you want it badly, and this style of horn is of the never-failing kind and is always ready for use. The signal is so sharp and penetrating that it demands and receives immediate attention from any person who happens to roam in the way of your car. Nickeled bell. Other parts, black enameled. Shpg. wt., 13 lbs.
2K2807 Hand Klaxon. Price, each............ **$7.00**

Heavy Tone Horn

$1⁸⁹

2K2806 This horn has a heavy, far-reaching tone, is simple in construction, and, with the brackets that are supplied with it, can be screwed to the side of the seat in a very convenient position. It is made of heavy brass, finely polished. Length over all, 13 inches; diameter of bell, 5 inches. Bulb of the finest quality. Shipping weight, 2 pounds.
Price, each...................................... **$1.89**

Horn Tubing

We carry in stock extra flexible, air-tight horn tubing. Made of brass, finished in black enamel. Average shipping weight, 1¼ lbs.
2K2794 Horn Tubing, ½-inch, 40 inches long.
Price, each.................. **65c**
2K2795 Horn Tubing, ½-inch, 50 inches long. Price, each...... **80c**

Jericho Exhaust Horn $4⁰⁰ Up

Only horn that will effectively blow when your engine is at slow speed. Deep toned, though soft and melodious when exhaust is light. Speeding up engine very rapidly increases volume of sound without losing melody. Just the horn for con-

Two-Tone Chime Horn $2¹⁰

2K2805 This horn has a tone entirely different from the ordinary bulb horns. Its volume and quality, although far-reaching, is very pleasing to the ear. Two reeds are harmoniously tuned at different keys. Made of brass, finely polished, with the best grade of horn bulb, and dust screens in each horn tube. Length, 15 inches. Shpg. wt., 2½ lbs.
Price, each.................................. **$2.10**

Big Value Auto Truck and Motor Boat Horn $6²⁴

This mechanical horn requires no batteries, wires, bulbs or other parts that need constant attention. Not affected by dust, oil or water. A pull on the handle makes sufficient sound of deep, penetrating power that the individual instinctively moves AT ONCE. Has screen in mouth to protect it from dust or dirt. Handsomely finished in nickel and black, or all black. Shipping weight, 9 pounds.
2K2802 Hand Horn, black and nickeled. Price, each................................... **$6.24**
2K2803 Hand Horn, all black. Price, each....**$6.24**

Chains, 6c Up

These are genuine case hardened cross tensile strength. They will kind of wear.

	Shpg. Wt.	Price, each
inches	4 ounces	6c
inches	6 ounces	8c
inches	6 ounces	9c
inches	7 ounces	10c
inches	7 ounces	12c
inches	8 ounces	15c
inches	9 ounces	18c

Michelin Type of Tire Fork

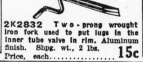

2K2832 Two-prong wrought iron fork used to put lugs in the inner tube valve in rim. Aluminum finish. Shpg. wt., 2 lbs.
Price, each. **15c**

Fastest Quick Detachable Tire Tool on the Market

24c

2K2833 Will easily and quickly remove tire without cutting or gouging. Won't scratch or deface wheel, and will fit any size tire from 3-inch to 5½-inch. One of the most important tools you can own. Made of best malleable iron, aluminum finish. Shipping weight, 1¼ pounds. Price, each. **24c**

Steam Vulcanizer
For Casings and Inner Tubes

98c

This excellent Vulcanizer will save you a large sum of money. Even only one repair on a casing will repay you, through time saved and the increased mileage of your casings. Punctures, small cuts or stone bruises are bound to occur, and if not promptly attended to, will fill up with dirt and cause blow outs. Usually two tools are necessary to take care of both inner tube and casing work, but this one will handle the two. Simple of operation. Does not require gauges or thermometers. Can't over-heat. Flame enclosed, thus insuring absolute safety. Handy for road use. Will make repairs without the necessity of deflating or removing tire. Wind does not affect flame. Comes packed in a substantial box, complete with chain, hook

Vulcanizing an Inner Tube

Biggest Value of the Day

bolts, thumb nuts, roll of repair gum, measuring can, sandpaper and full instructions for using and saving yourself many dollars. Adapted to all casings and tubes. Very finely made. Will last a lifetime, always giving the service that you might expect from a vulcanizer that you would pay $5.00 for. You will not make any mistake by sending for this one today. We guarantee that you will be pleased and we guarantee the article. Shipping weight, 6 pounds.

Vulcanizing a Casing

2K2727 Steam Vulcanizer. Price, complete................ **98c**

Vulcanizing Stocks 18c up

To get satisfactory results from any steam, electric or gasoline vulcanizer, it is absolutely necessary that you have the best material obtainable for the purpose. We offer here the highest quality repair stock to be had at these prices.

2K2760 Tread Stock, in small cans. Price, per can		18c
2K2761 Tread Stock, in ¼-lb. rolls. Price, per roll		38c
2K2762 Tread Stock, in ½-lb. rolls. Price, per roll		62c
2K2763 Tube Stock, in small cans. Price, per can		18c
2K2764 Tube Stock, Red, in ¼-lb. rolls. Price, per roll		38c
2K2765 Tube Stock, in ¼-lb. rolls. Price, per roll		38c
2K2766 Tube Stock, in ½-lb. rolls. Price, per roll		62c
2K2767 Fabric. Best 14½-oz. Egyptian Cotton Duck, treated on one side. ½-pound rolls. Price		$0.74
2K2768 Fabric, as above, in 1-pound rolls. Price		1.40

For shipping weight, add ½ pound to each above.

Strongly Made Tire Irons

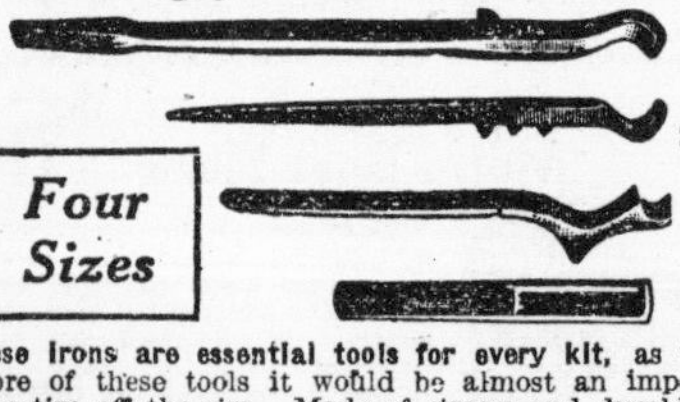

2K2828
2K2829
2K2830
2K2831

Four Sizes

These irons are essential tools for every kit, as without one or more of these tools it would be almost an impossibility to get the tire off the rim. Made of strong and durable malleable iron with aluminum finish. Can be used for either clincher, clincher quick detachable or straight-edge casings. Made in four sizes as illustrated.

	Shpg. wt.	Length		
2K2828	2 lbs.	16½ inches.	Price, each	18c
2K2829	1½ lbs.	13 inches.	Price, each	15c
2K2830	1¼ lbs.	11 inches.	Price, each	15c
2K2831	1¼ lbs.	8 inches.	Price, each	10c

Auto Emergency Mud Hook

78c

Will Fit Any Size Tire from 3 to 6 Inches

One of these mud hooks on each wheel will get you out of any mud, sand or snow. Unlike chains, they can be attached to the wheel after it is already in deep mud. Two or three pairs can always be used to advantage. Made of the best malleable iron, black enameled. Will fit any size tire, from 3 to 6 inches. Complete with straps. Average shipping weight, 3 pounds.

2K2735 3-inch or 3½-inch tire. Price, each pair........ **78c**

2K2736 4-inch or 4½-inch tire. Each pair.......... **78c**
2K2737 5-inch or 6-inch tire. Each pair.......... **78c**

The New Shaler Safety Vul-Ki

$3.24

2K2728

Small enough to carry in a tool box. Automatic in operation. Temperature cannot rise above vulcanizing point. No watching, no regulating. Fill the puncture or cut with new rubber, clamp on the vulcanizer to tire or tube and light the generator. The fuel supply is limited to that required for perfect vulcanization. You cannot overcure or undercure a repair. Tubes are clamped against the vulcanizing surface by a swivelled plate inlaid with asbestos to retain the heat and prevent pinching the tube. Handle, always cold, permits removing vulcanizer from tire as soon as repair is finished. The fuel is denatured alcohol, eliminating smoke and soot. Gasoline may be used if desired. There is no danger of spilling burning fluid on a tire. The fuel is enclosed in the generator, not kept exposed in an open cup. It is furnished complete with repair material, everything but the fuel. Shipping weight, 7 lbs. Price, each................ **$3.24**

The Brown Impulse Tire Pump

2K2850 Operates on the compound principle, inflating the tire with absolutely pure cool air. The special breather valve has a tension of 3 ounces, the ordinary motor having about 5 feet of vacuum. The atmospheric pressure of 15 pounds to the square inch immediately overcomes the vacuum, and the pure air rushing into the cylinder takes the place of the gasoline vapor. In other words, there is less resistance in the breather valve than in the gases from the motor.

The cylinders are made of gray iron, bored and reamed on special machines. Only one set of pistons are employed.

To operate the Brown pump you simply give the top of the spark plug, which we furnish with the pump one quarter of a turn and lift the center electrode from the plug. When you have the pump in place you give it a one quarter turn and it is locked gas-tight, ready for use.

Complete, with quick detachable spark plug, 12 feet of air hose, accurate recording gauge and self-opening hose connections. Full directions with each pump. Give size of your spark plug. Shipping weight, pounds.
Price, each **$10.75**

Weed Non-Skid and Rid-o-Skid Tire Chains

$2.40 up

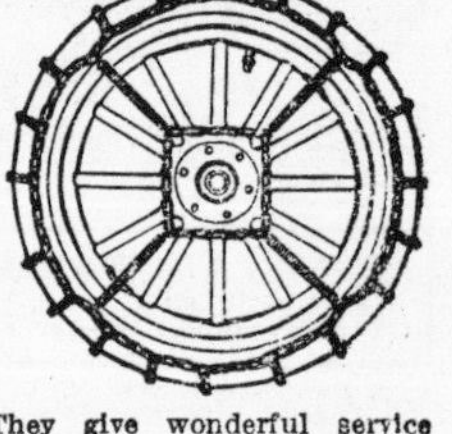

These anti-skid chains are indispensable for motoring in all kinds of bad weather. They give positive traction under the most trying conditions of either mud or snow interference. All parts are treated to prevent rusting, and the cross chains are case hardened to give additional mileage. The Weed Anti-Skid Chain is everywhere recognized as one of the most effective safeguards against skidding to be had. They are simple in construction, and can be quickly and easily adjusted. Rid-o-Skid Chains are manufactured to meet the demand for a chain of good quality at a moderate price. They give wonderful service for the price asked. Each put up in a strong cloth sack, delivered free to any part of the United States. No matter how effective the anti-skid on your tire may be, it is not half so effective and secure as the Weed chain.

	Size	Shpg. Wt.	Price of Weed Non-skid	Price of Rid-o-Skid
2K2500	28x3 in.	12 pounds	$4.00	$2.40
2K2501	30x3 in.	12 pounds	4.50	2.50
2K2502	32x3 in.	13 pounds	5.00	2.60
2K2503	30x3½ in.	14 pounds	5.00	2.65
2K2504	32x3½ in.	15 pounds	5.50	2.80
2K2505	34x3½ in.	15 pounds	6.00	2.95
2K2506	30x4 in.	15 pounds	5.50	2.80
2K2507	31x4 in.	15 pounds	6.00	2.90
2K2508	32x4 in.	16 pounds	6.00	3.00
2K2509	33x4 in.	16 pounds	6.50	3.10
2K2510	34x4 in.	17 pounds	7.00	3.20
2K2511	35x4 in.	17 pounds	7.50	3.30
2K2512	36x4 in.	18 pounds	7.50	3.40
2K2513	34x4½ in.	17 pounds	7.50	3.40
2K2514	35x4½ in.	18 pounds	8.00	3.50
2K2515	36x4½ in.	18 pounds	8.00	3.60
2K2516	37x4½ in.	18 pounds	8.75	3.75
2K2517	36x5 in.	21 pounds	9.00	4.50
2K2518	37x5 in.	22 pounds	9.75	4.70
2K2522	37x5½ in.	25 pounds	13.00	5.40

New York Electric Tail Lamp

$1.27

2K2890 **This Electric Tail Lamp has** become very popular. It is designed to match any style of front lamp. It fits either flat or round brackets. The front is ruby corrugated glass and there is a bent heavy plain glass on the side. Fitted with electric connector and socket; 6-volt 2 C. P. Mazda bulb. Finished in black enamel. You can light up from your seat. Shpg. wt., 1½ lbs. Price, each...... **$1.27**

Electric Tail Lamp

$2.49

2K2891 **A lamp which will meet all requirements of state laws and city ordinances.** Suitable for all makes of cars. Extra size semaphore ruby lens. Equipped with special cut out plug or switch, which conforms to certain state laws. Fits round or flat brackets. Electric connection and socket. 6-volt, 2 C. P. Mazda bulb. Diameter, front, 3⅞ inches; diameter of ruby glass, 3¾ inches. Shpg. weight, 1½ pounds. Price, each........ **$2.49**

The Famous Oil Tail Lamp

$1.86

2K2895 **The light gives the very best of** service. An efficient lamp in every way. It is used on cars of all kinds and descriptions. It is constructed of heavy gauge brass, with positive locking oil pot and perfect ruby semaphore lens, 3 inches in diameter. The side glasses are 3 inches and the lamp is 10½ inches high over all. Tail Lamps always burn. Black and nickel finish. Shpg. wt., 3½ pounds. Price, each **$1.86**

Round Oil Tail Lamp

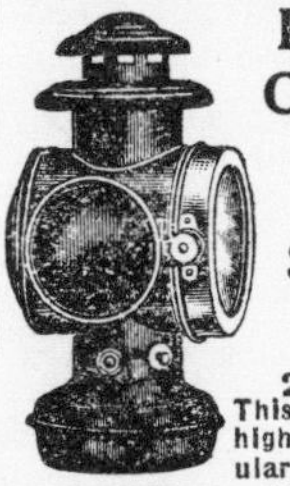

$2.04

2K2897 **This lamp is a high grade popular size.** Has never failing cold blast construction, is suitable for all cars, and is guaranteed to burn steadily for 24 hours. Made of heavy gauge brass, finished in black and brass. The doors are finished brass and riveted. Patent safety oil fount catch. Fits round or flat brackets. Height, 9 5-16 inches. A very satisfactory tail lamp. Shpg. weight, 3 pounds. Price, each.......... **$2.04**

Plain Gas Tip

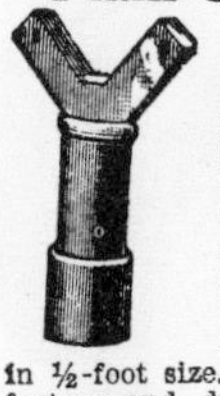

2K2910 **This acetylene gas tip or burner is a domestic lava** of unusually good quality. Made with standard base and furnished in ½-foot size. A very satisfactory and durable tip and one that will prove a money saving value. Shipping wt., per pair, 5 oz. Price, per pair.......... **9c**

Fine Gas Tip

2K2912 Same as our **No. 2K2910,** except that it is made from German lava, a material which will give highest efficiency. A great favorite with autoists on account of its low price, lasting qualities of size of the flame. Made in ½-foot standard base. Shpg. wt., pair, 5 oz. Price, per pair...... **21c**

Matador Gas Tip

A popular burner giving a wide, fan-tail light. Tips are made from German lava, a material which has been found the best. Carried in 6-inch and 9-inch sizes. Shpg. wt., per pair, 5 oz.

2K2913 ½-foot. Price, per pair.......... **21c**
2K2914 ¾-foot. Price, per pair......... **21c**

Fancy Gas Tip

2K2911 **This number, known as the Hexapillar,** greatly improves the appearance of your lamp. It is made of German lava, which has been proven to be the most satisfactory material for gas tips. Burners tested to the standard and fully guaranteed. Made in ½-foot standard base. Shpg. wt., per pair, 5 oz. Price, per pair.......... **24c**

Gas Tubing Fittings and Two-way Cocks **7c**

Strong, durable and inexpensive cast brass fittings for connecting rubber generator tubing to as many parts of the car as you wish. Sets of these fittings should be in every automobilist's repair box.

2K2905 **Straight.** Shipping weight, 4 ounces. Price, per pair.................... **7c**
2K2906 T Way. Shpg. wt., 4 oz. Per pair.......... **7c**
2K2907 4 Way. Shpg. wt., 4 oz. Per pair.......... **7c**
2K2908 Y Way. Shpg. wt., 4 oz. Per pair.......... **7c**
2K2909 2 Way Cock. Shpg. wt., 2 oz. Each........ **15c**

YORK AUTO TIRES ARE POSITIVELY GUARANTEED TO DO 3,500 MILES

$9.00 Gas Headlight

2K2870 **This is the Improved type of Close Coupled Flare Front Searchlight.** There is no light more powerful than the gas headlight. Because of its simplicity of operation it will always have thousands of friends. It embodies all the latest ideas in the art of lamp making. The body of the lamp is drawn from a heavy gauge of sheet brass. The 7-inch short focus mangin ground mirror is so placed that all light is thrown directly in front of the car. The diameter of the flange is 10⅝ inches, giving the front a bold and massive appearance. Extreme length is 7⅝ inches, and extreme height is 11 5-16 inches. The distance between the props is 7 9-16 inches, and the props are so firmly fastened to the lamp that there is no danger of their falling off or being shaken loose. Finish is fine black enamel with brass or nickel front. Shipping weight, 15 pounds. Price, per pair......... **$9.00**

Gas Tubing

2K2903 **This grade of red rubber gas tubing for use on automobiles,** has been found to be the most durable and satisfactory obtainable. We carry it in ¼-inch size, which is standard. Shipping weight, per foot, 2 ounces. Price, per foot.......... **7c**

Pump Tubing

2K2840 **We carry only the best grade of pump tubing.** Made of several plies of fabric and of such strength that it will not burst under 125 pounds pressure. Will fit all standard pump connections or nipples. Will outlast any two section of hose that comes with your pump. Put on some good hose now. Shipping wt., per foot, 6 oz. Price, per foot...... **8c**

Metal Lamp Connections

2K2875 **Made of flexible interlocking ¼-inch leak proof brass tube.** They are fitted with heavy rubber ends, having a metal base; these connections cannot become porous and leaky. Shipping weight, 4 ounces. Price, each.......... **15c**

Rubber Lamp Connections

2K2874 **Our rubber lamp connections are made of a grade of rubber** which has by actual test been found to best withstand vibrations without breaking off. They have extra large ends, reinforcing the point receiving the most vibrations. Shipping weight each, 4 ounces. Price, each.......... **10c**

Gas

2K29
little t
every n
cycle or
uses gas
made t
burner
dirt wh
cumulat
burns th
off the
which is
machin
2 oz.

CHAPTER IV

19

25

Sedans, Swank and Slush...

T HE decade following World War I seemed auspicious: America had "made the world safe for democracy." Demand for American products exceeded supply. Wages were high, profits enormous. Optimism and opulence filled the air. Nowhere was this more evidenced than in the automobiles of the period. Already a solid American institution, the motor car now became a thing of comfort and beauty. Designers outdid themselves creating a distinctive body type. Engineers added outstanding mechanical improvements. There were long, low limousines for the plutocrats, sleek Bearcat racers for the flaming youth and utilitarian all-closed models to take the proletariat to work. The majority of American families acquired a car in this decade. Never again did enthusiasm run quite so high. It was the golden age.

To children growing up in the 1920's, it was a different world than their parents had known. Distance had been annihilated. No one thought a whit about driving fifty miles to a party or a dance. There was no longer much question of mechanics and breakdown. Cars were built to run. Their powerful motors, coupled with improved roads, were a tremendous stimulus to unbridled speeding over hill and dale. Crashes became more and more frequent. Fond parents worried at home while Junior sparked his girl in the auto. A boy now had to have one in order to find out whether the girl was worth taking to the altar. Clergymen crusaded against the evils of petting and necking in the sedan. Chaperones were almost a thing of the past. "Parking" and "Out

Sorry I can't give you a ride downtown. Junior and his girl left the back seat out in the park last night.

Is **that** what they mean by "parking?"

Is that a car I see on the hill-top?
Yes, darling, but must we try to pass it?

of gas" stories filled the magazines. Peter Arno's famed cartoon showed a bedraggled couple coming to the park policeman with the rear seat cushion, and wanting to report a stolen car. Everyone seemed agreed that, more than anything else, the automobile was responsible for a change in morals.

And what of the actual cars that lay behind all this uproar? The variety of makes was not nearly as great as in the preceding decade. Still, there was a goodly number; 134 to be exact,—of which only thirteen survive today. Most every one who was riding for the first time in the 1920's remembers the common cars, Maxwell, Willys-Overland, Chevrolet, Dodge. But what of the real aristocrats of the period: Brewster and Locomobile limousines, luxurious Pierce-Arrows and Premiers, the swank Stanley Steamer and the Franklin air-cooled job, the glass enclosed "showcase" electrics—also dubbed "floating greenhouses"? What of those long racy Appersons Jackrabbits and Stutz Bearcats? What of the Marmon, the Moon and the Chalmers? Gone are all these, but not forgotten yet in legend and song. The song "Take Me Out in a Velie" means something special to certain of today's matrons and the story of "His Unreliable Pilsiner" still makes the rounds of Fraternity House Row on alumni week.

A single phrase can be used to characterize many of the bygone cars of the 1920's decade—Beauty and Craftsmanship. Here the car came to look like a car; fenders designed to give the idea of speed, bumpers front and rear, good body lines to cover the motor, bodies built around the driver— bodies he could enter with ease and sit in comfortably. One might reminisce about universal application of electric starters reliable heating and cooling systems, good brakes and new type springs. Few, however, would be interested. The thing everyone remembers is the color and eye appeal of these cars.

The early 1920's, which brought the closed sedan model to the lower priced field, will more likely be recalled as the hey-day of low slung open roadster jobs. Such is fame. Here was the dawn of the all purpose, all weather family car, yet do we look back to these forebears of today's two-door neces-

1928 BUICKS, now advertised with "Body by Fisher"—promoted with the phrase: "when better cars are built Buick will build them."

A 1928 FRANKLIN. Its body lines won the acclaim of designers.

1929 CHRYSLER 77 phaeton, with tonneau cowl and windshield, was billed as a "new first for thrill collectors," sold for $1,795 F.O.B.

The CHRYSLER 80 Imperial, advertised with the slogan, "as fine a car as man can build." It cost $3,595.00 F.O.B. Detroit.

LINCOLNS of 1928. Wire wheels, which packed full of mud and snow were having their day. "Artillery" wheels—the wooden spoke kind which were inherited from carriages—were by then obsolete enough to be considered something swank and special.

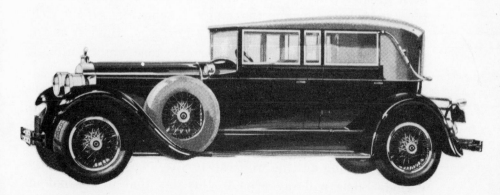

PACKARDS of 1927-28. When doughnut-shaped tires first appeared, people said they would never work. But by this time they were demanding balloon tires and the disk wheel. Demountable rims were long past. If you had a flat tire you now changed wheels.

sity? No! We wipe a tear from our eye for an impractical car type that is lost to us—and gone forever.

Few people ever owned an open roadster in the 1920's for the simple reason that these babies cost between $3,000 and $6,000. Yet who then riding does not get a vicarious thrill at the mere mention of their archetype—The Stutz Bearcat. Mention this car to a man now in his forties and he is likely to start off on a train of reminiscences from which there is no stopping. . . . "Ah yes, I remember one time." Thereupon follows the wierdest set of free associations one could ask for . . . coonskin coats . . . maiden names of women long forgotten . . . road houses . . . their bands and their songs . . .'I Might Be Your Once In A While'. . .the hip flask. . .articles of clothing lost . . . and, of course, the dashing way the thing got over the ground . . . seventy-five miles an hour . . ."the Stutz Bearcat. . .yes indeed."

If one tries to recall the person who actually owned a Bearcat back in 1920, he is likely to draw a blank. After frantic searching through memory files, the best he can usually do is decide that so and so probably had one. "He must have had one," they finally decide, "He was just the type."

Just the type! Certainly a very special kind of compliment is being paid a car to have it represent a type of occupant. Phenomenal when you realize that the swank Bearcat sang its swan song in 1925 and that the car has not been manufactured now for a quarter of a century. Of course, the even greater compliment is that this car, in representing a type, will ever remain the single, exclusive, self-sufficient symbol of a manner of living—The Jazz Age. Have it as you will, this car seemingly stands for a bygone way of life and the people who lived it.

The Stutz Bearcat and its time are inextricably linked. It stood for fast swank—with emphasis on the fast, for both car and occupants. It was seductive looking to the eye, swung low and painted red or yellow, with the newly invented Klaxon horn sending out the wolf call to strolling "dames" of the period. Some will say even to this day that it was not an

In the lush '20's, social life centered around a swank motor car. Heydey of "The Beautiful and Dammed"; Do you know the car?

In this decade the rural service station became—and often still remains—the center for dispensing all kinds of information from road conditions to news reports and local gossip.

The Bearcat was often snapped at World War 1 flying fields, complete with officers and cognac.

Russell Patterson's drawing (Holiday '48) recreates the swank of the Stutz Bearcat era.

The Bearcat was seductive to the eye, but its bucket seats were chaste enough in design.

The Bearcat hero delighted in making spectacular campus entrances accompanied by some reigning movie queen.

The Bearcat will remain the self-sufficient symbol of a way of living forever gone.

especially fast car on the road and that its bucket seats actually preserved morals by setting up a little wall between occupants. But legend is to the contrary.

The Bearcat crowd (even though they actually traveled in Mercer Raceabouts and Apperson Jackrabbits) were the gay insouciant lost generation. They were in high school while their older brother fought the war, came home disillusioned to set the stage for "Flaming Youth." They were the young and fun loving, the beautiful and damned of story and song. The boys belonged to such dreadfully secret societies as Skull and Bones and The Twelve. The girls all played favorites and spent their life in a continuous round of parties and proms. They truly loved the Stutz and its cheaper imitators. Tin Lizzies were cut over to look like snappy chariots. But nothing could really take the place of a true racing car. It looked full of fight, fun and frolic. No top? Who cared! When it rained or snowed, the occupants let it—and risked pneumonia. "Eat, drink and be merry, for tomorrow we die."

Just as the Bearcat stood for a "lost type" in that bygone decade, so the sedan—the closed car—stood for the future. There had been closed car jobs before the 1920's but these had been popular only as a second car for the very rich. Everyone—rich and poor alike—wanted an open car, so they could tour in the open air. When they could, they had a Marmon or Stearns-Knight. If they could not afford these touring models, they would settle for a Ford.

The idea of a closed model for the one-car family dawned slowly, was in fact hampered by the expensive gadgetry and fine hand coach work that characterized the first limousines. Yet had it not been for these early forebears, the sedan of the 20's would not have become the comfortable, all-purpose car that eventually captured most buyers' eyes.

Aristocratic limousines, from which all closed cars are descended, were popular from 1910 to 1935, with peak developments about midway in the passage. This hectic time of war and false prosperity saw the rise and fall of a special art form—the period car. These ostentatious and custombuilt

Evolution of the closed car. At the top, a 1906 Pierce Arrow, at the bottom a 1916 Locomobile Laudaulet. The all-closed sedan did not arrive till a decade later.

Vivid, intense, authentic in its application of curite hues

A MINERAL so modern as curite finds a most fitting counterpart in this La Salle Roadster, an essentially new, vigorous, timely motor car. The Ledge Orange and Ravine Yellow of body panels, fenders, and mouldings parallel the striking color series so intense in the stone; and the upholstery in genuine pigskin carries the same tones— a striking effect which is further emphasized by the instrument panel in bright Orange Duco. The striping is Watercourse Red.

La Salle Roadster

BODY BY FISHER

An emerald, platinum mounted—a possession to prize, to adore

Fenders, running board aprons, and the slatted valance on top of the gasoline tank are finished in Argent Duco to supply the platinum mounting for this Emerald Green Cadillac Sport Phaeton. Color unity is preserved by upholstery in Emerald Green leather, which also edges the carpet, the top boot, the trunk cover, and the storm curtains. Equipped with double cowl, tonneau windshield, and searchlight mounted on a nickeled stanchion on the right running board, the car is captivating in its vigorous beauty.

Cadillac Four-Passenger Sport Phaeton
BODY BY FISHER

"There is nothing quite as impressive of elegance as the exposed Chauffeur,"
—so ran a Locomobile ad of the early 1920's. Even before that, other American makes had begun to ape this affectation from the foreign car salons.
A period piece and gone forever.

jobs cost from \$7,000 to \$20,000. They were produced in small quantities by master coach builders, and such as survive today are gems worthy a king's ransom. They boast rosewood paneling, richly figured upholstery fabrics, cut glass flower holders, silver and gold door hardware by Gorham or the Tiffany Studios. The limousine became popular as soon as the electric starter, multi-cylindered engines and high grade springs gave the automobile chassis enough poise and power to carry a fine coach job with appropriate dignity. It was ushered out in another twenty years when the effects of the country's worst depression made ostentatious cars unpopular, if not impossible.

Those were the days when the annual motor salons in New York, Chicago, London and Paris were brilliant society events. In foreign salons fine American chassis like Lincoln and Dusenburg would be shown fitted with the most sumptuous Paris and London coachwork. In America, since foreign cars were banished from the New York automobile show, importers established a special salon just to show the imports. The absence of fine car imports during World War I was a tremendous stimulant to American coach builders. From 1925 to 1935, when the foreign salon idea was all but abandoned, a number of jewel-like creations were paraded before the public eye. Newspaper files of the day recognized the following list of ultra-class American limousines: Cadillac, Chrysler Imperial, Cunningham, Dusenburg, Franklin, La Salle, Lincoln, Locomobile, Marmon, Packard and Pierce-Arrow.

Since custom coach work and functional design just about joined the lost arts by the end of the decade, the 1920's will always be remembered by many as the car's greatest age. Cadillac, whose "Body by Fisher" became a "class" label, boldly announced (1929) one of its creations as "an emerald, platinum mounted, a possession to prize, to adore." Almost overnight even the middle class touring car trade became body-beauty conscious, began to clamor for popular priced covered automobiles. The sedan, sired by wealth, now moved into the low price range and stayed.

Malcolm Bengay, editor of the Detroit Free Press, once said. "Henry Ford put the world on wheels and the Fisher Brothers covered it." Though not literally true, there is enough fact behind that line to make it stick. Ford's successful marketing of 15,000,000 Model T's of unchanged design made him the most fabulous individual in automobile history. And that there ceased to be a Model T in the mid 20's is due in large measure to the Fisher body works.

How did this come about? The public, of course, had not lost confidence in the Model T's superiority as a cheap form of transportation; but they now wanted something in addition to a vehicle that covered the ground. By 1925 everyone was well convinced that the automobile was good; and once convinced of that, they also wanted it to be good looking. The Model T definitely did not qualify in that category, whereas some of Ford's competitors had begun to move their styling into line with the beautiful creations of the upper price brackets.

Ford held out until 1927, when Model T sales had slumped from 1,655,076 units to 450,230 units, all in a year's time. This was the year when Chevrolet, with a dependable motor and a nice closed body line outstripped Ford. He was never again to recapture leadership in the lower price field. His Model A lasted only three years, when there was another change to the V8. Why? Though he never admitted it, Ford was responding to a cold hard fact: the American public now required beauty as well as utility in all its automobiles.

Behind this shift in public taste stand the Fisher Brothers. Though their auto bodies were never used on the Ford, it is sufficient that their advertised catch phrase "Body by Fisher" had set a new standard in body style and comfort. The Chevrolet approached this standard more nearly than did the Ford.

Where did it all start, this American development in distinctive auto coach work? The first concession of automobile manufacturers to line and beauty appeared in the Oldsmobile curve dash runabout of 1900-1905. This was such an improvement over the horseless carriages, which were little more than a buggy box mounted on a frame, that buyers began to

138

Ford's Model A and Willys Whippet are now only memories.

demand models where attention was paid to body line. That brought the carriage and coach makers into the automobile game. The two largest were Studebaker Corporation of South Bend, Indiana and the B. F. Everett Company of Detroit. Everett received so many orders for what were called "Auto Bodies" that he developed the Wilson Body Company to take care of the overflow. And to the Wilson plant he introduced the Fisher Brothers, seven young men who had learned their trade in their father's shop at Norwalk, Ohio. Soon the brothers were to start a body concern of their own and soon also to produce the first four door touring model, immediately adopted by all car manufacturers and the sensation of the 1910 decade. The year 1925 found them busy making glass enclosed sedan bodies for all weather use, making them better and more cheaply than other competing concerns, and making more and more money for themselves. Their eventual rise to power in General Motors, with a dominating block of stock in the corporation is another story. Here it is sufficient to indicate that their development of body designs had as much to do with popularizing the auto as did the engineering developments of other men.

They did not do all this alone, the Fisher Brothers. They were not even the first with many body improvements. But they somehow learned to build a beautiful, sturdy body by mass production methods, and reaped financial reward and fame from this fact. More specifically, it was their ability to fabricate closed sedan bodies at half the original anticipated cost that brought this style, presumably possible only for high priced limousines, to the low priced field. By the late 1920's closed models were offered at no great premium over open touring models on all makes of cars.

A further factor entered into the popularity of closed models, other than their growing beauty of line. The public had become interested in the all weather car partly because more and more use could be made of the vehicle for daily business purposes. Consider what had been happening to American roads in the decade since 1915. As more and more

This advertisement, appearing in 1925 financial publications, marked marraige of automobile production to Wall Street finance.

people bought cars, louder and louder became the clamor that something be done about cross country highways, and arteries of traffic leading into cities. Barely more than lanes in many places, seldom gravel based, full of tortuous turns around old property lines, at the beginning of the century American roads were nothing to be proud of. People who travelled on business used the trains. The automobile was driven in a small radius for pleasure only. Now with steady road improvement, people began to use their cars for all transportation. Many moved out into the countryside and depended on the car to get them to work. A closed model was the logical choice for a vehicle that might be used every day of the year.

Whereas 1915 car owners were accustomed to put up their cars in winter, by 1925 this was an exception rather than the rule. Fairly complete interstate highway systems had been set up and elaborate machinery developed to keep them open in inclement weather. No longer was it necessary to ride carrying the Blue-Book of Roads on one's lap. There were signs telling which way went to Buffalo and how far away it was.

The cost of all this road improvement had been tremendous, but most of it had been paid out of the car owner's pocket. The state licensing of cars, first thought of as a safety measure, turned in a huge revenue as more and more cars took to the highway. Through their Associations and duly elected Congressmen these new car owners saw that much of their tax money went for road development.

The marriage of automobiles to roads led to all kinds of mutual improvement. But the greatest outcome, in terms of total effect, was the making over of Americans into a race of travellers, in just one decade. Until the 1920's millions in this country were living out their lives in horse and buggy radius of their birthplace. In 1910 it was always possible to find some old man who had not been more than ten miles from home since his return from the Civil War. In Brooklyn, you could find many people who had been born and married there and who had never travelled beyond the confines of Greater

New York. At the summer colony in upstate Watkins Glen, the families who met each other on the piazza of the old Glen Springs Hotel travelled only between their original birthplace and this resort, and that just once a year. Is it any wonder **that people conceived of Monroe as the name of a President rather than as a town that made a car?**

One decade changed all this. World War 1 had come and gone. Millions of Americans had been shifted all over the United States. Some hundreds of thousands of miles of improved roads now beckoned to be explored. Some millions of automobiles were ready to travel over them. So America took to the highway. City folk explored the countryside and fell in love with it. Farm families went to the big cities and fell into the habit of making their clothes and household purchases there instead of at nearby small towns. And travel kept up in bad weather as well as good. Demountable side curtains were not good enough for an all weather car to go to work in or to take in to town to shop. And so from this time on the sale of closed models rose, surpassed and eventually spelled doom for the open touring car.

What did they look like, these sedan jobs that the majority of car owners came to prefer to all other models? The popular priced lines included the Maxwell-Chrysler, Ford and Chevrolet and Willys-Overland, and are shown herein.

Who can remember when the Maxwell car suddenly became "The Good Maxwell?" That was when Walter Chrysler acquired control in 1921. This wizard of automobile management, fresh from his job of pulling Willys-Overland out of the post-war recession, now took the defunct and overexpanded Maxwell Company over at his own terms.. All he had to start with was a slogan, for this "Good Maxwell" was anything but good. Its rear axle had an annoying habit of folding up at the first chuck hole encountered; its carburetor was wheezier than most; and it had not kept up with changes in body style. When Chrysler took over, Maxwell was just another second-rate car in the crowded low-price field. It had 26,000 apparently unsalable units scattered among dealers in all parts of the

CHEVROLET

57376

Bigger and Better

1928

A
Sensational Achievement in Beauty and Performance

Marvelous new bodies by Fisher . . . longer, lower, and roomier . . , and styled with all the artistry of world-famous designers! A 107-inch wheelbase . . . the longest ever offered in a low-priced automobile! An improved valve-in-head engine . . . smooth, powerful and swift in acceleration! Four semi-elliptic shock absorber springs . . . permanent assurance of delightful riding ease! Non-locking four-wheel brakes . . . powerful, dependable and velvety in operation! That's what the Bigger and Better Chevrolet offers you—at prices so low that they are actually amazing! Small wonder that everyone calls it a sensational achievement in beauty and performance! Small wonder that it is everywhere hailed as the world's most luxurious low-priced automobile!

CHEVROLET MOTOR COMPANY, DETROIT, MICHIGAN
Division of General Motors Corporation

Q U A L I T Y   A T   L O W   C O S T

country. If a dealer managed to sell a Maxwell, the purchaser might be back the next day with a crackup, and the dealer-organization was itself cracking up under accumulated strain. On advice of advertising counsel, Chrysler launched the "Good Maxwell" slogan to offset the psychological barrier to purchase. And while building a new car that would live up to the slogan, Chrysler got the 26,000 unwanted cars braced up, marked down and sold out. Next year and the next, more and better Maxwells rolled onto the highways. But somehow, even though the Maxwell had become a good cheap car, the public never accepted it to the degree it took to Chevrolet and Ford. So in 1924, again on advice of advertising counsel, Maxwell production ceased and a newly designed car was trundled out bearing Chrysler's own name. From here it was but another step to Plymouth, a stable new contender for honors in the low price field.

Consider for a moment, the economics of automobile manufacture in 1925. The post war depression of 1921 had shaken the industry down into a more conservative business than it had ever been before. Hundreds of small and insufficiently financed concerns had failed. Competition was shaping up between three large car combines that would eventually cover all price ranges, General Motors, Ford and Chrysler. One by one the independents not in these combines began to drop out. What was left of them in 1929 was about wiped out in a newer and greater depression. The industry was no longer a free-for-all, but a small group of monopolistic companies.

The low-priced car field became a battle between two outstanding names in 1925, Ford and Chevrolet. Ford had never had any really challenging competition till his former employee, William Knudson, was now elevated to the presidency of the Chevrolet Company. He promptly took a large portion of Ford's business, so that the last half of the 1920's decade belonged to Chevrolet as surely as the first half had been Ford's—so far as cheap cars go. Plymouth did not make its appearance until 1930, and the public in this era of false prosperity were turning more and more to higher priced cars.

Ralph Barton's (L. M. '30) The Very Latest. Detroit manufacturers produce an automobile so low a human being can't get into it.

Want to get married do ye? Better stop over night, have the announcement printed in the sassity column and get some tire chains so you won't do any skidding on the slippery road of life. (Werner, '20.)

Each manufacturer of cars in the high-priced brackets spent the time before the 1929 crash in trying to out-do the others by placing a showy nameplate on the car to stamp it with the maker's individuality. Cost of the plate was no object in years when competition was at its fiercest. Some concerns developed distinctive statuettes and radiator ornaments that are works of art. These and the car lines themselves make of the late 1920's an era of truly lush motor cars. Long, low and sleek of line, they will forever stand for lush spending, the day of the bootlegger, the plutocrat who lighted his cigars with five dollar bills, and the mechanic who wore silk shirts to work.

It is fitting that the cars of this bygone lush era had loud commanding voices. Early automobiles used weak bulb horns to announce their approach and retirement from the scene. In most cases no horn was necessary, since their vigorous chugging and backfiring heralded them from afar. Later on some cars were equipped with an elaborate disc music box that played a special tune. But the electric horn, or Klaxon, which came in with the 1920's, did away forever with the Beep-Beeps and Tinkle-Tinkles in automotive warning signals. In 1925 the German Bosch horn became preferred to the earlier Klaxon and practically all lush cars of the era switched from Klaxon's characteristic Ka-hooga! to the Bosch's penetrating beBEEP! Soon Trumpet Horns were available for those who wanted even more deep-throated refined noise, the Cow Horn for those who thought a bovine bellow was a smart trademark. Whether from the newness of the horn creations, or a desire to call attention to the ostentatious motor car itself, drivers "laid on the horn" in this era more than at any other time. Thus the period of swank and slush is ushered out with a harsh and never to be forgotten sound.

148

PERIOD PIECE

Of 134 makes of cars on the market in 1920, only those noted in capital letters below still survive.

Ace	Common-	Hollier	Mitchell	Roamer
Allen	wealth	Holmes	Monitor	Rock Falls
American	Crawford	HUDSON	Monroe	R. & V.
Anderson	Crow Elkhart	Huffman	Moon	Sayers-Six
Apperson	Cunningham	Hupmobile	Moore	Saxon
Auburn	Daniels	Jackson	NASH	Scripps-
Austin	Davis	Jones	National	Booth
Beggs	Detroit	Jordan	Nelson	Seneca
Biddle	Dixie Flyer	King	Noma	Singer
Birch	DODGE	Kissel	Norwalk	Standard
Four Davis	Doris	Kline	Oakland	Stanley
Bradley	Dort	Lafayette	OLDSMO-	Stearns
Brewster	Dupont	Lexington	BILE	Stephens
Briscoe	Elcar	Liberty	Overland	Stevens-
BUICK	Elgin	LINCOLN	PACKARD	Duryea
CADILLAC	Essex	Locomobile	Paige	STUDE-
Carroll	Fergus	Lone Star	Pan	BAKER
Case	Ferris	Lorraine	American	Stutz
Chalmers	Fiat	Maibohn	Paterson	Templar
Champion	FORD	Marmon	Peerless	Texan
Chandler	Franklin	Maxwell	Piedmont	Tulsa
CHEVRO -	Gardner	name	Pierce-Arrow	Velie
LET	Geronimo	changed to	Pilot	Vernon
Cleveland	Grant	CHRYSLER	Porter	Vogue
Climber	Halladay	McFarlan	Premier	Wasp
Cole	Hanson	Metz	Ranger	Westcott
	Harroun	Mercer	Raulang	WILLYS
Comet	Haynes	Milburn	Reo	Winton
Columbia	H.C.S.	Meteor	Re Vere	

CHAPTER V

19

35

Jalopy Fever....

WE have come to the years of Depression. The great days of 1929 and its false prosperity are now only memory. Men who bought those expensive luxurious cars of halcyon days have either committed suicide or are still sitting in dazed stupor wondering how they can recoup vanished fortune. Meanwhile Life and the Automobile go on. It is the day for rediscovery of the common man and the common car. Vast federal works projects sired by the "New Deal" take up the slack in employment. People are trying to get to places where new dams and superhighways will be built with public funds.

How do they travel? By auto, of course, the entire family and all their living equipment besides. The bedspring is laid on top the car roof, the oil stove is parked on the front fender, the insides are bursting with kids and bedding, the tea kettle and other leftovers are tied to rear bumper. What cannot be attached to the car proper is tied to a home made trailer and hitched on behind. One would hardly recognize the makes of the cars themselves. They are largely old cars from the former lush decade, sedans with cracked windows, dented fenders and weird paint jobs. Many carry crudely painted signs: "Leaping Lena," "California Here I Come," "Enter Here with Can Opener." Even the new cars have a raffish, offhand look. People sing songs entitled "Tumble into a Rumble," "Take Troubles Away on the Highway" and "Depression Glide." Everyone tries hard to make light of straightened circumstance. College boys tinker with wrecks from the junk yard, consider it smart to drive around like a

152

Alan Dunn's automobile cartoons for New Yorker have delighted thousands. The upper dilemma needs no caption.   courtesy N.Y. '36.

New Yorker

Alan Dunn

Know any place around here I can get my car greased?

"hick." A method is discovered to siphon gas from the service station pumps when attendants are home asleep in bed. The wind blows up the dust bowl and the Okies take off for the West. Most everyone is uprooted, looking for work. It's the day of Jalopy Fever.

Many car companies were casualities of the depression. While the solidly financed "Big Three," Ford, General Motors and Chrysler, skidded along with 90% of the limited new car business in their hands, the independents were largely frozen out of the declining market. Most, like Marmon, failed completely. A few, like Studebaker, recovered after terrible agonies. Comparative case studies of these two concerns show that one had what the other lacked for survival. It was not money—which neither had—but men.

Look first at the Marmon,—once famous name now vanished from the highways. If you drove one of these cars twenty or thirty years ago you were probably wealthy, and certainly lucky. Wealth was involved in the purchase of a Marmon, because here quality was never sacrificed to price and luck came thrown in, for the car was one of the most dependable on the road. The first Marmon had come out in 1902 with many advanced engineering features; and within ten years a Marmon won the first international sweepstakes 500 mile race at Indianapolis Speedway. This "greatest sports event in automotive history" made Marmon famous overnight. From there on it continued its wide-spread popularity until the stock market crash dried up the usual kind of buyers Bank loans were called and the company folded. Why did it not make a fight for life? Largely because its management were engineers, not supersalesmen. They tried to make a car right and expected it to sell itself. It never was fortunate enough to interest a sales genius who might guess what a buyer's market would take and tailor the product accordingly. Instead, its management might delay production to install some new improvement, thereby missing the chance at the few sales that might be made in depression years. It lost its dealer support and is thus only a racetrack memory.

Now look at Studebaker, an independent that goes stronger than ever today. Studebaker had from the first a supurb sales organization, had in fact that organization, long before it had an automobile to sell. And it was a sales organization, not its engineers, that pulled the company out of its near-crack-up in 1933.

Practically everyone knows that Studebaker began as a carriage concern with its product known throughout the world. Studebaker went into the automobile business in 1902 as a sideline. Within ten years its salesmen were selling so many cars the carriage plant could not work fast enough putting motors and parts bought elsewhere into the bodies made by themselves.

To supply demand, the Studebaker sales organization took on the sale of the E. M. F. automobile on a country-wide basis. Now began a highly costly maneuver by which Studebaker acquired for $7,000,000.00 control of the E. M. F. organization and its automotive engineering brain power including Walter Flanders of earlier Ford fame. Things went well until the 1920's when Studebaker's new president, Albert Erskine, decided to enlarge the Studebaker line, make it a rival to General Motors. He first attempted to get into the low-priced field with Ford and Chevrolet, but his new Erskine car ran head-on into the depression. Always an optimist, Erskine thought that expansion could be made a way out of depression. So he acquired working control of Pierce-Arrow—one of the highest priced cars on the market and already dying a slow death from lack of sales. Then he attempted to launch in 1930 a new low priced car, the Rockne, named after the famous Notre Dame coach. This also failed. No one much was in a position to buy a new car in that year, let alone a new and untried model. All conservative automobile makers were taking to the storm cellar, making only slight pretense at fixing new lines or introducing yearly model changes. In 1933 Studebaker liabilities exceeded quick assets by some $15,000,000.00. Erskine bowed out by putting a bullet through his brain, and

The depression 30's are sometimes recalled as the era of the College Hick. Old cars, painted with all types of slogans—from the mild "Enter here with can opener" to the raconus "Bad odors to the rear," created many a campus problem. Some colleges banned student automobile driving.

thereby created an opportunity for the most spectacular comeback in automotive history.

The great accomplishment by which Paul Hoffman and his associates saved Studebaker was essentially one of salesmanship. Hoffman was already in the Studebaker organization at the time of the crash, a Vice President in charge of sales. And it was he who sold the Studebaker receivership on the unique idea of spending more money to keep production going and the sales organization alive. Powered by a new model and dealer enthusiasm for its competitive pricing, Studebaker then sold its way out of the depression, kept thousands of people at work when other factories closed down. It went into the war years as a newly reorganized company—fit as a fiddle and ready for defense contracts.

The importance of dealer enthusiasm and drive was never more evident than during the 1930's, when every car sale was a major victory. Shopping about in that buyer's heydey is a memory some will always cherish. Even before it became apparent that the shopper had a steady job and could therefore purchase a car on time if he wanted, he was literally taken off his feet with courtesy, seated sumptuously and shown by an elaborate chart-talk the very special features of the Ford, Chevrolet, Studebaker or whatever make the dealer featured. Listening to such a sale talk, one became convinced that for all practical purposes a new Ford was faultless as a Lincoln, a Plymouth just a small version of the Chrysler and the Chevrolet as classy as a Cadillac. The strange part was that the salesman believed his own argument—else he could not have been so convincing.

Coming up for air, often with a copy of a signed car order in his hand, the dazed customer might wonder wherein the source of the salesman's persuasive power. It came, of course, from the crowd psychology of the dealer's annual meetings. In this show of new models, banqueting and briefing for sales campaigns, men were stirred to a frenzy of enthusiasm for the car they represented. Pep talks by men who had chalked up notable sales records despite the depression made others eager

ANTAM

LINCOLN-ZEPHYR

PLYMOUTH

CHEVROLET

GRAHAM

THE 1938 MODEL

ON PA

AMERICA'S FAV

BUICK

DE SOTO

PACKARD

DODGE

OVERLAND

OLDSMOBILE

CADILLAC

FORD

MERCURY

RADE

ITE INDUSTRY

LA SALLE

LINCOLN

NASH

HUPMOBILE

STUDEBAKER

UDSON

PONTIAC

CHRYSLER

to hit the sawdust trail. Carried away with a self-induced hypnotism, many did go forth to do or die for dear old Henry or Plymouth or Stude. What if their enthusiasm did transcend the facts. All cars produced in the 1930's were good cars. And if a customer could be sold a Whosis on the dubious assentation that its upholstery could be cleaned with a wet cloth, there was another customer who would fall for a Whatsis car simply because it was supposed to save most on oil. All in all, justice was fully served.

The truth of the matter is that all the major automotive improvements were already in by the early 1930's, the electric starter, hydaulic brakes, demountable wheels, all-steel bodies. One can go through an almost endless succession of automobile "firsts" and find that little or nothing fundamental has been done to improve them in the intervening years. Streamlining, of course, was tried out on a tentative scale in some 1930 cars. But that it met with little interest on the part of the public is shown in the early demise of the first air-flow Chrysler—a butt of period jokes and now a collector's item because so few were made and sold.

Oh, there had been a new air-cleaner for the motor. But who really cared any more for slight improvements. Well then, try something the public appreciated, something that would make its present cars seem antiquated, crimp the body steel a new way, shift the headlights and doorknobs around, add the chromium trim and convince anyone not having these additions he was not fit to be driving in public. Induce the buyer to go into debt if necessary to get a longer wheelbase with the talking point of greater riding ease. This last really got some people away from the old jalopies. Throughout the 1930's there was a mad scramble among manufacturers to see each year which could put out the longest car, long not in terms of life value but in inches. The car that could stick out its bumper an extra inch was tooted to the skies by its dealer impressarios. The public was urged to look upon its overall and buy, buy, buy. Many were impressed by the 1930 cars, but relatively few could put the money on the line.

160

1936, "The Royal Family of Motordom." Top to bottom: CADIL-
LAC for $1,645; LaSALLE for $1,375; FLEETWOOD for $2,445.

Nothing was wrong with sales appeal, and at no time in the history of automobile manufacture could one get as much car for the money. In 1905 the average price of an automobile was $2,137.00, F. O. B.; in 1935 it was less than $800.00 delivered. It was simply that one had to eat first. Besides, the cars of the lush 1920's were still good cars.

One could get a really good used car cheap, especially if upkeep was not figured. This period saw the flowering of the Used Car Lot. On South Michigan Avenue in Chicago there were seeming miles and miles of cars for sale, and Detroit had even more of these emporiums. The better cars predominated, tagged with almost unbelievable resale prices. In 1935, a friend stopped to take a long look and came away in possession of a 1929 Lincoln phaeton, complete with real leather seats, hidden compartments, special glass windbreaks and countless chrome plated gadgets, all for only $65.00. When you consider that this hardly covered the original cost of one of the two spare tires carried in fender tire wells and that the car listed at around $5,000.00, you get some idea of how far the bottom had dropped out of the class car market. This particular car had belonged to a man who went broke in 1930, and it could do better than 75 miles an hour. The only drawback was that it took as much oil as it did gas to run and that twenty-five miles of transportation cost in the neighborhood of around $7.00. At this rate, it is easy to see that some used cars were no bargain at any price.

Demand for used cars continued brisk until the late 1930's. Many families without jobs surrendered the equity in their homes, acquired a used car and constructed a trailer of sorts and took to the highroad. Okies moved from their dust bowl to the California fruitlands, Negroes in broken down Packard limousines migrated North, New England Yankees moved to Western centers of building and industry. Some mechanics, seemingly tired of chasing about for work, settled down at some crossroad hut or abandoned hot-dog stand, hung out a sign "Garage" and went into business repairing other people's jalopies that happened to pass his way.

162

"Bear", shrieked the supercargo suddenly.

"If you're seen in town again, this mark means you'll go to jail.

Best of the books popularizing automobile travel was F. Van de Water's THE FAMILY FLIVVERS TO FRISCO, with typical scenes illustrated above.

There is little doubt that the ease with which parts could be found for the popular cars, Ford, Chevrolet, Buick, contributed to their widespread use in traveling. Some dealers almost supported themselves on their spare parts business during these years. Men who never tinkered with their own cars before did so now of necessity. As one's confidence increased, he might start working on other people's old cars. It is said that the number of repair shops trebled in this decade. It must have been fairly lucrative too, this business of fixing asthmatic jalopy sufficient to send it rolling on its way under its own power, charging the ever hopeful owner a few dollars and wishing him Godspeed to the next repair bill.

It is hard to see where many people got the money to keep their cars running. Somehow they did. It was about the last possession a family would give up. Even when food was being supplied by government dole, it was not uncommon for some to swap their food coupons for enough gasoline to get them out on the highway for a spin.

The weekend joy ride had become a national institution. Cross country traffic increased by leaps and bounds. The number of people making their homes in cars was a matter of national comment. You could not get folks to give up their urge to travel. Against all good judgment, many poured good money after bad to keep their wrecks of cars still running. They had jalopy fever.

The public's love for cars that had seen better days took some bizarre forms. Peculiar color combinations were splashed over once swanky sedans. Slogans reminiscent of rah-rah college days were employed by many owners who had hardly seen the inside of a grammer school. Rubber mudguard flip flaps and all kind of dime-store gadgetry were used to make the old cars seem new.

Many more could decorate the outside of an old car than could open the hood and discover the slight quirk that kept the thing from running. Millions of persons driving could not tell the difference between a crankshaft and a camshaft, between planetary and sliding gear transmission, between a piston and

164

Streamlining: The Early and Late of it.

Drawing of Chrysler's 1933 AIRFLOW model. It was not a popular success.

"The Blister Six," A Raymond Loewy projection into the future.

Please Don't Be My Valentine

Stanley Stamaty and
Clara Gee Kastner

DREAMING DONALD

You think you own the road! Alas,
Your motto is, "They shall not pass!"
Of what, dear Donald, do you dream,
While you dam up the traffic stream?

SUICIDE SAM

For you who pass upon the hill
And leap the double line,
I vote most likely to succeed
As no one's Valentine.

HONKING HORACE

You who honk at yellow lights
Are something of a heel,
Offending those with better rights
Behind a better wheel.

The Safety Cartoon. A recurrent theme of the 1940's. (Courtesy Ford Times.)

a pet cock. Of the one hundred fifty million people able to drive after some fashion, less than half could now make the simplest repair. As for the more knowledgable half of the drivers—to say nothing of pedestrians—these were lucky indeed if the uninformed group could even distinguish between the accelerator and the brake.

The combination of deteriorating cars and poorly oriented drivers was, in fact, beginning to get out of hand in the 1930's. Consider how accident figures crept up. In 1910 about 3,000 auto fatalities were reported annually. In 1920 the number had risen to 12,500 a year, in 1935 to 36,000. The clamor for licensing drivers and compulsory insurance now began to be heard. Wrecks and accidents became more and more frequent. It took the publicity of the famed Readers Digest article "And Sudden Death" to move the country even a little way to traffic control safety. Drunken drivers and underage youth were forbidden from driving; but the menace of the poor vision and the slow reflexes of old age has remained to this day without legislation.

It has always seemed a marvel that Americans, so naturally mechanical, came so quickly to forget the essential nature of the gas buggies their genius had sired. Even in nursing their jalopies through a depression, there was not as much owner repair of cars as at the beginning of the century. People had become used to the notion that what went on under the hood was not their affair, a matter for specialists.

What went on under the hood and floor board had by this time come to be taken for granted, until everything stopped. Then let the garage man worry about it. And if one became discouraged by almost constant repair bills, get the thing to a used car lot, trade it in for another that seemed to run better. No one knows how much the public was gyped by its inability to diagnose motor ills. Reader's Digest ran a set of articles telling how motorists were charged for repairs that were not made, how poor cars were traded in for worse. The only thing folks seemed conscious of was external differences in cars. They could tell a 1929 model from one of 1935,

"Would you mind waiting till the battle scene to drive in?"

"There goes one of those old fashioned streamlined jobs"

Today's cartoonists lampoon the old as well as the new in cars.

also the difference between a 1935 and a 1938 Ford. "Oh look at the new Ford," they would say as one drove by, "see how the hood extends over the radiator grill. . . . No it's not a '37. Last year's model had the radiator grill coming up a little higher."

"And there goes the new coopay."

"You mean coop."

"Well, what's the difference how you pronounce it; you see what I mean, don't you? Isn't it snappy."

As the decade wore on and the depression wore itself out, more and more people began to trade in their old jalopies for new cars. It finally became obvious to the majority of motorists that it was cheaper to trade in for the bargain-priced new models than for over-priced used cars. Jalopy fever had by now run its course. Under the threat of war, industrial production was again moving into high gear. With more money in his pockets than he had had for a long time, the factory worker turned to buy—usually "on time"—a new car. So the old cars began to be abandoned, the cars whose straight fronts and visored windshields now seemed as old fashioned as the Gibson Girl. Some were left in the barn under piles of hay. Others were used as chicken roosts, or cut down for tow cars. A new period of somewhat uncertain prosperity was getting underway. The motoring public rushed into it, driving farther and faster than ever.

The owner's version of his Car   Ours

CHAPTER VI

19

40

Scrap for War...

W E have come to 1941 with America at war. Old cars that had literally been falling by the wayside in depression years suddenly acquired new and special value. Scrap iron was a precious commodity and broken down automobiles provided plenty of it, with lots of brass and chrome thrown in for good measure. Back and forth across the countryside went the junk dealers paying premium prices. The haul was tremendous—Ramblers and Wintons from the 1900's, Model T's from the 1910's, Stutz Bearcats and Marmons from the 1920's, Chrysler's experimental "air-flow" sedan from the 1930's, and many other makes of less historic interest. Even the "doodlebug" assembled from parts of several cars, was brought in and broken up. Patricians and plebians of former days made their last journey together to the blast furnace and oblivion.

Oddly enough, few mourners marked the demise of the relics of the nearby past. Here and there, of course, an old couple parted reluctlantly with the Peerless in which they took their honeymoon, and a farmer wiped away a tear as he pulled the hay off his first Ford and let it go for good and all. Such sentimentalists are no match for national emergency! A treasured memento weighs no more than an abandoned derelict in which the chickens roost.

Factors other than high scrap prices helped to pry old cars away from their owners. Many who needed cars to get to their war work were eager to turn in the barnlike bodies

"Anyway, here's the emergency starter he sold us with the car."

and wheezy motors of earlier decades in favor of the newer and faster streamliners of the 1940's. As for those whose use of a car was not rated "essential to the war effort," the restrictions on mileage, and rationing of tires and gasoline was enough to discourage continued ownership. Why not turn it in, save garage rent and upkeep, and have a brand new car after the war was won. Even a man's first car love, out of service for years, was not immune. In the pull between personal nostalgia and patriotic enthusiasms, the latter won by a wheelbase.

We will never know how many thousands of old cars were fed into the maw of war. But the reduction in motor traffic is indicated by maintenance figures. It is estimated that the yearly cost of car servicing operations was reduced $100,000,-000 during the war years.

Not all cars, of course, were driven off the road by travel restrictions. If one could not get to essential work otherwise, and if he agreed to pick up as many riders as could hang on the sides, a reluctant board of bluenoses would dole out some precious gas coupons. Under sufficient pressure, doctors could even buy a brand new car from the precious supply of 1941-1942 models that the government confiscated when the motor makers ceased production and retooled their plants to turn out airplanes, anti-aircraft guns and tanks.

What a hey-day the junk yard would have been for an old-car enthusiast during the war years. Unfortunately, most of these would-be collectors were occupied with other things elsewhere—at Guadalcanal, in Africa or a desk in Washington. Unattended, many a museum piece was broken up and gone forever. It is significant that in tracing the genealogy of certain 1940 models, we are today largely dependent on old advertising pictures rather than on photos of extant specimens. Look at a few genealogies and see the tortuous road over which various families of cars have come.

Consider first the Chevy, the most popular car of the decade. Product of General Motors, it achieved that combina-

Through the year's PACKARD has fought to keep its distinctive radiator front. Can you identify the model numbers and years of the cars shown?

tion of value so dear to the American heart—class, dependability and low cost. Matters were not always thus.

The drama of Chevrolet goes back to 1910, when W. C. Durant—the man who put the General Motors Corporation together, first evinced an interest in a light car that was struggling under production difficulties at Flint, Michigan. It had been designed by Louis Chevrolet, a French racing driver whom Durant had known since the days when he sold him a Buick car. Durant saw in Chevrolet's new gadget a chance to compete with Ford in the cheap car field.

He formed the Little Motor Company to manufacture Chevrolet's model and sell it at $650.00. In 1913 he bought another tiny motor concern, the Republic, at Tarrytown, New York, and combined the two as the Chevrolet Motor Company. The first Chev came on the market in 1913. Its success was phenomenal. First with an unique air-cooled motor, then with more and better features than Ford's Model T, it eventually outstripped its rival. Durant, who had earlier lost control of General Motors, was now able to get back the helm by taking his new creation into the combine. In effect, within two years after its debut, the little Chevrolet Company had swallowed big General Motors. And though Durant again lost control through personal bankruptcy in 1936, his "sweet little car" has never lost its hold on popular fancy or its place as kingpin in the General Motors set-up.

Consider next the Plymouth; its genealogy is tortuous. Plymouth began as the Maxwell, and before that it was the Briscoe. The Briscoe-Maxwell began back in 1903 when John D. Maxwell, a mechanic who had helped put together the Hayes-Apperson and Oldsmobile models, brought a new radiator "cooler" to Benjerman Briscoe and asked for a price on its quantity manufacture. Briscoe owned the largest sheet metal plant in Detroit at that time and had already caught autobug fever. He said to Maxwell, "If you have a new radiator design, why not go ahead and build a car around it —our car." The result, better looking than the Ford, sold quite widely; elated by such easy success, Briscoe organ-

nameplates on this page are a small
part of the collection of Harry W.
Bell of Wellesley Hills, Mass., which
numbers well over 1000 plates.

They have been displayed at the
Museum of Science & Industry in
Chicago and the Golden Jubilee in
Detroit.

Twice FRANKLIN has changed from its shoeshape radiator, only to return. Note radical design shifts of 1900, 1910, 1920, 1930 for this air-cooled car.

ized the U. S. Motor Company, a combine of 150 concerns. U. S. Motors ambled shakily along, manufacturing 28 different models until it collapsed under its own weight in 1912. From this debacle, only the Maxwell was salvaged. It went into a new combine with the Chalmers-Detroit, but was soon in financial difficulties in 1920. Once again it was rescued, this time by Walter P. Chrysler. We have already seen how Chrysler rechristened it "The Good Maxwell," and made the car live up to the name. But in 1925 it was decided that the ghosts of previous financial and mechanical failures made the Maxwell name more liability than asset. First as a low-priced Chrysler, then, in 1929, as the Plymouth, Maxwell again emerged to command a place in the low-priced sun.

Will Plymouth stay? From its war years it emerged a very weak third in the "Big Three." But Plymouth, nee Maxwell, still has many friends who would never think in terms of another car. And as Maxwell always managed, Plymouth will undoubtedly amble along.

Buick. Now there's a name in cardom! With us from the first, it has enjoyed almost fifty years of uninterrupted popular favor and financial stability. It and the Oldsmobile were the first stars in General Motors crown. Early known as the "a good car," it stands today—as in 1903—for what some call "middle class smugness" and what others call "content." Can Buick's rise to high place in popular demand mean that more Americans are becoming smug and content? Only in outer trappings, presumably. Americans have always bought big looking cars when they could afford them.

Note now the Nash. Back in 1901 it was the Rambler Runabout. Shortly thereafter it followed Columbia and Winton to make a sensational advance in car design by moving the power plants from the rear to the front compartment for better balance. By 1914 Rambler was the Jeffrey, but still being made at the old stand in Kenosha, Wisconsin. Four years after this it became the Nash, as the former President of Buick and General Motors decided to move out on his own. Nash has pioneered some mechanical improvements, but will be chiefly remembered for folding beds for travelling tourists. When this first came out, in the 1930's, other manufacturers watched public reaction with an eagle eye. If this became the popular way to tour, it meant all others would have to follow suit. But Johnny Q. Public did not like especially the idea of trying to sleep in his car on tour. For one thing, it was always too crowded with suitcases, spare tires and souvenirs. There was no place to let the bed out unless the contents were disgorged outside. So he took to trailers and road side camps, and preferred the Nash because it was just another good car.

You have only to look at the forebears of today's Jeepster if you want a frenetic genealogy. It started back in Indianapolis in 1903 as the Overland, with a super New York promotor, John Willys, buying up the company's entire yearly production for a $10,000 advance payment. The company was caught in the financial panic of 1907 and would have folded after the manner of other fly-by-night concerns, except that Willys determined to save his investment by what was very high finance in that day. Stalling off creditors daily, he got out 500 cars in 1908 and sold them at a profit of $50,000. Next year, credit improving, he took over the Pope automobile plant at Toledo, Ohio, formed a new company to market an entirely new automobile, the Willys-Overland. The year 1916 saw this car in its heyday, and also the man who made it. Absence of good management (due to Willys absorption in war work), overexpansion of inventories at inflated prices, and a disastrous seven months strike brought the company to its knees financially. The banking groups, to whom was owing nearly $50,000,000, got Walter P. Chrysler from General Motors to pull the Willys out of the hole. The result, carwise, was a completely new model, a cheap little 4 cylinder job. As this snub-nosed "puddle jumper" lurched along, making and losing friends, management was shuffled and reshuffled. Then, largely because its factories were not busy and could be more quickly retooled, the Willys company got a lion's share of the Army's Jeep orders. Although the Jeep was partly a Ford development, Willys won from its war work a priceless

From JEEP to JEEPSTER. Willys-Overland advertisements show which way the market lies.

name with which to make a new try at the civilian market. The Jeep was first advertised as the postwar farmer's car, its four wheel drive could take it over any ground, plow fields, or pull a bogged cow out of the muck. Relatively few farmers, however, fell for the Jeep. Instead, it became the darling of postwar high-school youth. Catering where the demand seemed to lie, the Jeep lost its curious high-cocked appearance, took on a tin station wagon body, eventually turned out the swank Jeepster sport model. This Willys found itself much favored for short hauls,—a far cry from the days when it was the Overland . . . billed as the easiest riding car made.

One could go on similarly with cars like the Packard, the Hudson, and the Studebaker; they are about all that remain from the hundreds of models once made. Who remembers the little Brush Runabout, with its chain drive and gear shift lever pivoted outside the wooden frame; it was once billed as "Everyman's Car," and had wooden axles and coil springs that are today items of collector interest only. Who, too, has ever seen the Stanley steamer busses that once took passengers up and down mountains, paused by a roadside brook to refill the boiler, then puffed off again,—a veritable locomotive on wheels. These relics of the 1910 era made good scrap, so too such 1920 casualties as the Saxon, the Durant and the Rickenbacker, such 1930 bygones as the Rockne and the Essex—the latter especially dear in memories of rocking needed to unlock its frequently stuck starter. Many of these cars were found only in parts, a wheel here, a fender used to repair some other car, a radiator there.

Searchers for historic auto parts were the first to work over the graveyard of dead automobiles. As early as 1920, a few "queer ducks" began to look for varieties in auto horns, hubcaps, and head lamps. They paid a small premium over scrap prices and stripped these relics from the old cars with their own hands. The remainder of many a museum piece was broken up. Junk dealers estimated their value by weight alone.

We must not forget that the practice of stripping old

1900. "It's safer to have a horse along if power fails you,"

Some years later: "Oh, for a horse!"

It's a l-ee-tle old fashioned; but the only car old Shep can run under.

Ford Times.

"He checked her stem to stern, and found only those two tickets we misplaced for the Teddy Roosevelt Rally." Even though Model T had long since disappeared, it was still a joke in 1948.

cars until there is nothing left of them has long sanction in America. Many an early mechanic built his first car out of parts acquired from a variety of broken down factory products. And in the first quarter of the century, many people tried to get a few more miles and wheezes out of a car no longer manufactured by writing all over the country in search of replacement parts. An early source of supply was Alfred Dunk in Detroit. From the panic of 1907 down through the 1930 depression, this man assisted in liquidating more than 700 automobile concerns, his theme song becoming—Defunct, Junk and Dunk. When the samples and spare parts were not taken over by a new company, Mr. Dunk usually bought them for resale to stranded motorists throughout the nation. This was a real service, but it failed to save many old cars for posterity. In the end, its owner gave up the struggle to keep it running, decided instead to keep up with the Jones', turn the old car in for something new.

As much happened to motorists as to their cars in the war years of the 1940's. There was a loss of interest in auto racing, a shift of many families to nomad existence and the tourist court, a change in hitch hiking habits and a growing fondness for gimcracks and gadgets to bedeck the family chariot.

The passing of widespread popular interest in auto racing was more than a war-time casualty, it was a sign of the full coming of age of an industry. No longer could the auto be considered a plaything or freak. Anyone with enough gas and a good car could well approximate racing speeds on the highway. Mere thrill seekers began to flock to other sports, such as ice hockey. When in 1945, a group of veteran race drivers, headed by the ace Eddie Rickenbacker, sold their interests in the Indianapolis Speedway, the big day of auto racing seemed all but gone.

We may recall that auto racing began in this country with the Vanderbilt Cup contests on Long Island. Before World War I, these were conducted on the European plan; it was road racing, with irregular courses, sharp turns and

187

long straightways. After the war, private sportsmen's subsidies of such racing ceased and the sport shifted entirely to the strictly commercial ventures of the speedways. Now interest was shifting away from these contests, the sport falling far behind that of old-time horse racing in popular fancy. There were, of course, a number of die-hard enthusiasts of auto-racing; but in practically every contest, the foreign cars showed greater versatility and performance than did American cars; the latter were simply no longer built for racing.

If people tended to lose interest in watching others race cars, they were more avid than ever to go places themselves. The student of civilization can find no parallel to the quick change in the American scene that came with the automobile, good highways and widely distributed work. Almost overnight it changed the average American into a peculiar, restless, roaming individual. In 1910 cars were objects of conversation rather than travel. No wonder people conceived of Cleveland as the name of a President, not as a city they might explore for themselves. Millions lived out their lives in horse and buggy radius of their birthplace. Two wars and the automobile changed all this. Encouraged by such early sagas as Van deWater's "The Family Flivvers to Frisco," people took to the highways in ever increasing numbers. Five times as many cars crossed the continent in 1940 as in 1930, and 20 times as many as in 1920. The tourist business that developed to care for this movement was equally phenomenal. The real beginnings of the tourist auto court and the service station came in the early 1920's. In those times almost every town provided a free camp ground to take care of the auto migrants who were not being especially welcomed by hotels and townfolk. Finally as these public camp grounds became overrun with "tin can" tourists, some enterprising citizens began to erect shacks for which they would charge a small fee for overnight lodging. These grew more elaborate and more numerous with each passing year. Even during the depression they thrived because they offered cheaper accommodations than elsewhere. Public acceptance became complete by

188

THE PIERCE-ARROW CAR

takes a just credit and no more than a just credit for the quality of its engine, but it has added to that engine conveniences, refinements and luxuries which together with perfect service and easy control, give the luxury that is expressed by the words "Pierce-Arrow Car"

The Pierce-Arrow Motor Car Co., Buffalo, New York

1913

the second World War, when thousands of workers, soldiers and service wives took up permanent residence in tourist motels and trailer camps so as to be near their place of duty. The nomadic trend did not cease with the passing of the war. Seemingly, it had come to stay, making people more at home on wheels than anywhere else. The well appointed trailer house came to cost more than the car.

The war years saw a shift in the character of hitch hikers. Previously the standard member of this fraternity was a gentleman of fortune, out looking for new adventure. His tales were as exaggerated as Paul Bunyan's, but he was sure-fire entertainment—if one went in for that sort of thing. Such knights of the road were now replaced by energetic young ladies in slacks who travelled in pairs, on their way to earn fabulous sums working in war plants. Soon their ranks were joined by the boys in uniform, trying to make impossible mileage on short furloughs. Their stories—even when they'd been to war—were not freely given. And finally, at war's end, the hitch-hiker turned into the boy going to Cow College, purposeful and polite, but hardly companionable. There were, in fact, fewer and fewer pickups worth making on the road. The custom was all but dying out.

Absence of new car models left a gap for spending in the lush war years. Gadget hatcheries, however, cropped up at every hand. The old car could be tricked out with new visor, rubber mud-flaps, colored plastic gear shift lever, automatic cigar lighters, radio attachments and backing lights. In fact, almost anything that could be tied to the car from raccoon tail to gas aerator was sold in large quantities. Perhaps the purchase of these accessories helped assuage the lack of a new car. They certainly soaked up purchasing power, many of such poor material they did not last out the week. It must be reported also that the gadgets had little effect in making the old cars run better. One by one, these were retired from service or junked, the erstwhile owner deciding to save towards a postwar car instead of giving all his money to the omnipresent repairman.

CHAPTER VII

19

50

Return Engagement....

O VER fifty years have passed since the advent of the automobile in America. They have been fabulous years and it has been a fabulous development. We are in the era of the ballyhooed "post-war car." Of this designers, racing men and the public in general have expected too much. They compare its questionable point unfavorably with something that has gone before. The product is now old enough to have a history. People turn back the page with nostalgia and longing.

Collectors of old cars have appeared out of nowhere. The few specimens that miraculously escaped the scrap pile for war are now refurbished and restored with loving care. Horseless Carriage Clubs blossom over the land. A Grand Prix hill-and-dale run is staged after the manner of the old Vanderbilt Cup races. The Glidden Tour is revived. Any car more than twenty-five years old is now a museum piece. Radio and screen celebrities take up the hobby of old car collecting. They revive the old car songs. "In My Merry Oldsmobile" is once more a hit tune: "My Little Stanley Steamer" runs not far behind. Meets and exhibits are staged, with the jolly old cars huffing and puffing under their own power. The public flocks to see these early forbears of today's streamlined necessity play a return engagement.

This interest in the past is not difficult to understand. Look for a moment at the postwar car—"the last word in travel comfort" and, according to the copywriters, "The answer to everyman's prayer." It had not proven so.

Many a buyer of the "new look" in cars felt like a bride-

"Don't leave the ship, Mabel. Give me the tiller."

"And the policeman was so nice about it. He asked if I'd like the city to remove all the telephone poles."

Woman and the Car. The first witticism on this subject was made three minutes after a female took the wheel. Above is recorded early and late attempts in man's hopeless battle to keep the weaker sex from taking over his pet machine.

groom sold down the river. Once he had been sure that a flashily streamlined, chromium jawed, rocket car was the only girl for him. Now he awoke to the fact that she was very touchy inside and required expensive outer beauty treatments.

The first big gripe was over maintenance and service costs. Mechanically the new cars had been jazzed up to a point where they required the exertion of almost no physical effort on the part of the driver. Did he want to shift from high to low, he pushed a button—or the car shifted automatically as the foot came off the gas pedal. Did he want the window down—he pushed another button and it lowered under its own power. The instrument panel was a mass of buttons, radio dials, electric clocks, compasses and calendars.

It wasn't bad till something went wrong. Then it was bad indeed. On some models it was all but impossible to get the hood up and find the engine. On others the whole motor had to be unbolted before the crankcase could be removed. When the automatic lifters stuck, the entire car door had to be torn down to get the window back up. If the battery failed on some automatic shifting cars, it was impossible to start the motor by towing or a push. Cranking, of course, was equally out of the question. Even the detached hand crank had long since disappeared from the tool kit. The only recourse was a battery replacement brought in from the nearest garage. In their zeal to free the motorist from operational problems automotive engineers had overdone matters. The servicing of cars had become too complicated for the good of the owner's pocketbook. On body maintenance costs, many felt the new bodies had been purposely constructed to "damage easily and repair hard." Once a smashed fender could be removed by itself; now it was an integral part of the body panels and the whole side of the car had to be replaced. Fender installations costing under $20.00 for older models went up to $75.00 on certain postwar cars.

The rocket lines and widened bodies of the new cars had been accomplished only with annoying disadvantages to their users. Roofs were so low the average man had to take off his hat to sit down—a fact which Raymond Loewry—designer of the postwar Studebaker—caricatured with telling effect. Angled windshields gave better vision but also admitted more glare. Gadgets like the hand throttle and windshield visor— once standard equipment on all cars—were now being sold as accessories to alleviate new car difficulties. For short drivers who could not see over the hood, there were special lift cushions. Over and above all, the cars no longer looked like cars, but like guided missiles from Mars. Small wonder that public interest in new cars wore a little thin and that, by contrast, the "old look" seemed a "good look" indeed.

A market survey conducted by one of the leading automobile makers showed that people over thirty years of age did not care for the lines of the postwar car, compared them unfavorably with those of the late 1920's and early '30's. Younger folk, never having been exposed to the thrills of early car travel, thought the new rocket look quite appropriate to the atomic age. But young and old alike found much to interest them in the relics of the past, though for somewhat different reasons.

To those born into a world already transformed by the automobile, any survivals from its early days might as well be classed with the Declaration of Independence and the Sphinx of ancient history. Today's youth have no memories of the horseless carriage nightmares of the 1890's, the jolly, brass-bedecked runabouts of the 1900's, the Model T's of 1910 and the fancy racers and custom-built limousines of the 1920's. They were never pitched out the rear of a 1915 tonneau job or had a 1930 rumble seat close down on them as the car hit a chuck hole. They have never travelled miles and miles out of their way trying to locate a line of telephone poles that the Blue Book said would take them to town. To them a duster is something you use for cleaning, not something to keep your costume clean; a tarpaulin covers a haystack, not a car driver. Even the "side curtain" and "one man top" are archaic terms. What pleasure, therefore, to

CHROMIUM JAWED MONSTER

THAT ELUSIVE MOTOR

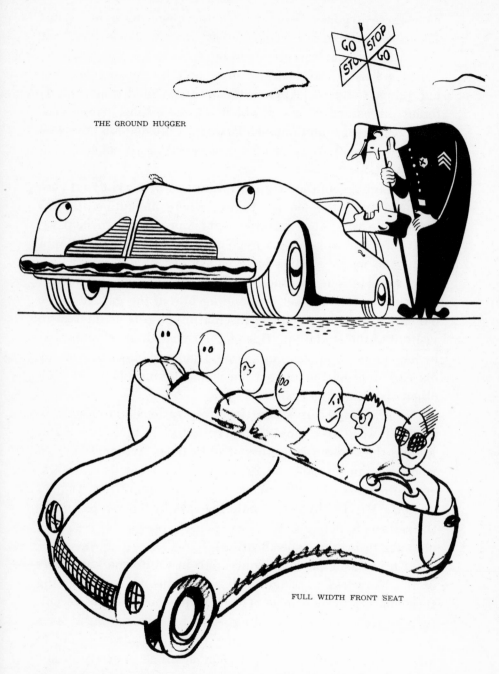

THE GROUND HUGGER

FULL WIDTH FRONT SEAT

RAYMOND LOEWY, famed industrial designer, takes 'time out' to lampoon post-war car design. (Courtesy Raymond Loewy Associates).

have these bygones brought back to wondering eyes. What fun to recreate an era when the car was not a necessity, just a plaything—the Merry Old Mobiles.

It is hard to say just how or when the interest in collecting old cars started. Apparently it caught hold in many different places and people at about the same time. Three geographical areas stand out—Hollywood, Philadelphia and New England, largely because of a concentration of collectors in those parts.

It might seem the original interest in preserving old cars stemmed from the movie studios, where an authentic 1905 automobile was often just the right "property" to help recreate the atmosphere of a bygone era upon the screen. As a result the major studios have collections of old cars which they rent to one another and to independent producers. Whether in use on a set or standing idle in the garage, these old cars are among the most fascinating objects of interest to visitors to the studio lot. One of their custodians reports that he has a hard time keeping people from climbing all over the old cars, tooting the ancient horns and taking photos of each other operating the crank.

Sparked by this studio interest, various individuals in the Hollywood area soon became collectors in their own right. Among the veteran collectors of old cars is Arthur Twohy, a wholesale lumberman, and Edward Miller, a car body designer, co-founders of the Horseless Carriage Club of Los Angeles in 1937. Mr. Twohy often rents his cars to the movies, using the returns to help pay for the expensive pastime of restoring old cars to original specifications.

Enthusiasm, as usual, runs high in California. Members of the Horseless Carriage Club are frequently seen nursing their charges to some meet. One old time motorist was recently arrested—not for speeding—but for obstructing traffic. These museum pieces come under their own power or not at all. And they may as well not come at all as to arrive in any but authentic detail. The trick is not so much to find an old car to drive as to restore it completely to the last taillight.

200

or Lohr of Chicago in an early Duryea.
Twohy of Los Angeles in a White Steam-
Jack Benny and his Maxwell need no
oduction.

Old carmania has taken Hollywood by storm. Walt Disney's production manager, Ben Sharpstein, drives a 1909 Patterson. (Courtesy
Sat. Eve. Post.)

The Horseless Carriage Club numbers many celebrities among its members. Edgar Bergen of radio fame keeps quite a few old cars and drives them. He reports that Charlie McCarthy is too much a smart aleck to be trusted alone in one of the ancient gas buggies. Edgar has, however, considered trying the Panhard out on Mortimer Snerd—it was originally billed as requiring no knowledge whatever for efficient operation.

Andy Devine of the movies, Zasu Pitts and her daughter, Ben Sharpenstein and Ward Kimball of Walt Disney studios are also collectors of old cars. Jack Benny does a lot of talking about his old Maxwell, but the Horseless Carriage Club would like to see him put in an appearance with the car actually running. The fact that you can operate the old cars instead of just looking at them is probably the most fascinating phase of this hobby.

Look now at the Eastern Seaboard for more fun and frolic. Recall that the first American gasoline automobile was made in New England. With this background it was only natural that a few Yankee folk began collecting old cars back in the 1920's. At first these were mostly stored in backwoods barns under piles of hay. But as more and more people caught "auto-bug fever," there was formed the Veteran Motor Car Club of America. The old cars were refurbished, taken out for road trials, and some were set up in museums open to the public. A leading light in the popularization of the old car hobby has been James Melton, Metropolitan Opera star, radio and movie entertainer. Mr. Melton frequently drives to out of town concert engagements in one of his rejuvenated old cars, and has now established the Melton Museum of Antique Autos at Norwalk, Connecticut. Another New England Museum is located at Princeton, Massachusetts, not far from the birthplace of the automobile. Still another is the Goyette Museum at Peterborough, N. H. Alexander Ulman and Ralph de Palma of race-track fame are members with a special interest in old-time racers. In and around New York City is another center of old car activity. Long Island already boasts

Old car museums have sprung up overnight.
two from James Melton collection at Norwalk,
Connecticut, and two from the Chicago Museum
of Science and Industry.

A scene from
"MAIN STREET—
THOMPSONVILLE"
as reconstructed in the
ompson Old Car Museum,
CLEVELAND, OHIO

The J. B. Van Sciver collection gives a complete history of the Stanley Steamer from the 1903 tiller-steered runabout and the 1909 boiler that required an engineer's license to the last model made—with the owner getting the steam up. (Top of page).

Mr. and Mrs. J. B. Van Sciver own a number of early luxury-class gasoline cars, including the 1909 chain drive Mercedes racer and the canvas-topped 1914 Brewster. Their trip in the 1909 Winton is slightly delayed while Mr. Van Sciver pumps a tire.

two museums, one at Southampton, the other at Centerport. One contains the Thomas Flyer of "round the world" fame. The Automobile Old Timers, Inc., made up of a group of pioneers in the business, was recently instrumental in getting the National Automobile Show to stage an exhibit of old cars along with the new models. By popular acclaim, the old cars outshown the new streamlined creations, stopping the show.

Last, but by no means least, accolades go to a group of Pennsylvania collectors, notably George B. Hughes, Paul Cadwell, Ernest Swigart, Thomas McKean, the J. B. Van Scivers, and their Antique Automobile Club of America. As an indication of how interest has grown in recent years, Mrs. Van Sciver points out that when they first caught the bug in the late 1930's, there were only about thirty-five members in this oldest of car clubs. Today there are over 1000 members. This association holds outings and meets every few weeks, its members arriving in dusters or tarpaulins according to the state of the weather. Widespread public interest attends these meets, and especially the Glidden Tour revival, which old car enthusiasts sponsor each year. On a recent Glidden tour run, it was practically impossible for national press photographers to get good pictures of the contest. All they could see of some of the most exciting parts of the "race" were the heads and backs of the throngs of roadside watchers. Interest in old cars has even grown to the point where one company is kept busy turning out miniature replicas for model builders.

California, New England and Pennsylvania, though long-time centers of old car mania, do not have a monopoly on this hobby by any means. Almost every month some new collector of automobiles, auto parts or automotive literature shows himself from Patagonia to Podunk. Chicago's Museum of Science and Industry boasts of a permanent exhibit called "Yesterday's Main Street." Against an authentic 1900 background are set the automobiles collected by Mr. D. Cameron Peck. This Chicago executive's collection of old cars began in 1939 with a 1912 two cylinder International Farm Wagon, whose high wheels were deemed well suited to the rutty roads

Automotive Postcards

Contestants for the 1903 International Race for the Gordon Bennett Cup.

of the day. Mr. Peck's inventory today lists over 130 automobiles, electric, steam and gasoline models, all in running
condition. Once asked to name his favorite, Mr. Peck replied
"It's an impossible question. I am like the Sultan of Turkey
with his hundred wives. I love them all."

Curiously, Detroit—the very center of the motor industry
—is not too well represented in the old car field. Everyone
knows the millions spent by Henry Ford to assemble the con-
glomeration of historic items that make up the Edison Institute and Greenfield Village. So it is a bit surprising to find
his collection of early cars not the most outstanding. B. W.
Pollard of Detroit has the largest collection of old cars yet
assembled, but there are few neighboring collectors. One will
meet more general enthusiasm by going down to Cleveland.

How does it feel to be an old car enthusiast? A Mr.
George M. Hughes has reported his own experience as follows:

"The year 1932 was the one in which the fatal Auto-
buggus bit me. The bite itself was of little consequence at the
time—just a mere scratch—but the effect was far-reaching. It
was a warm summer afternoon and I was walking down a back
street in a small town near my home in Upper Darby, Pennsylvania. A casual glance into an old private-garage building
disclosed a most extraordinary sight. Back in the corner was
an automobile long out of use. A close inspection revealed
the car to be a 1914 Buick four-cylinder roadster; in fact the
first model Buick placed on the market equipped with the
electric starting mechanism. Well, that was something!
The machine, despite deep layers of dust, was in excellent
condition, with low mileage registered on the speedometer.
After the hasty checkup nothing would suffice but an immediate attempt to buy the car. However, too much enthusiasm in
this effort aroused the owner's suspicions. Believing that he
had a goldmine on flat tires, he refused to sell. Thus it sat,
out of sight but not out of mind. I made many calls on the
owner within the next year, but he held out for a high price.

"Suddenly in June, 1933 an idea popped into my mind.
Why not advertise for an old car as people do for new auto-

mobiles? An advertisement was inserted in an Allentown, Pennsylvania newspaper. There were five replies. All were investigated and the search finally narrowed down to one, a Model T Ford which had rolled off the production line in 1915. The car was purchased for only a few dollars, and with considerable difficulty was taken home under its own power. Then came weeks of spare-time work restoring and reconditioning the car. One fine evening when all was completed there stood a glistening high-boy touring, ready for the road. My family heaved sighs of relief and clustered round to see me off on first "show-everybody" tour. From that day on, "Tin Lizzy" has periodically graced the roads in and around Philadelphia.

"Through 1933 and well into 1934 I played with the new toy. Then one of my routine calls on the Buick owner resulted in its purchase. Resistance had been worn down to a frazzle! The auto was towed home and eventually put back into running condition. . . . One might think that with two cars the flame would begin to die down; but it burned more fiercely than ever, especially when I found out from an obscure magazine that a man in Vermont had twenty-five old timers. From him I purchased a little Hupmobile 1910 roadster. The day scheduled for its arrival at my freight station found me waiting impatiently in front of the unloading platform. The 1914 Buick and some tow rope made up my equipment, as a multitude began to gather to see what was to happen. These provided willing hands for lining up the Hupmobile behind the Buick for towing to its new home.

"The second car acquired from Vermont was a 1910 Maxwell roadster. But now with four old cars on my hands, I had to rent larger garage quarters. Interest was rising instead of diminishing and by 1940 I had eleven cars. From then on there was no stopping me. The desire for motor arks and thunder wagons of a generation ago is as strong as ever. Such names as Duryea, Winton and Haynes are eagerly sought. I hereby give notice that a well-deserved and excellent home awaits any of these that come my way... Antique car collecting re-

First Stanley Steamer

1912 Steamer

1909 Mountain Wagon

quires travelling near and far, diplomatic and shrewd bargaining; but mostly it is work, dirty and greasy, and great fun. I can only say that to me and my kind the gleaming polished brass on one old, old car is more to be desired than all the chromium in Christendom!"

Probably no collector group come in for more good natured ribbing than the old car maniacs. This is because their hobby requires the open road and its attendant publicity. A housewife can confine her collection of early American pressed glass to her own cupboard, the stamp enthusiast can keep his books hidden in a desk drawer and the button collector can gloat over his buttons in private as he wishes. But part of the fun with old cars lies in driving them.

Naturally, if one is caught in duster and goggles, driving an old car along the country road or village street, he lays himself open to all kinds of remarks, both nasty and nice. He is a "funny guy," a "queer duck." And yet, as people come to see more and more of the old cars in use, they begin to have a respect and thankfulness for the old car collectors. Without their help, undoubtly, early physical specimens of the creation which—more than anything else—has changed the American way of life, would have passed into limbo.

Many of the old timers have disappeared completely at that. Where is there in existence today an Octoauto, where a 1901 Trimoto? Of many oldtime models we are lucky to have even a hub-cap, or a radiator ornament survive. Still, it is surprising how much of the past has been salvaged for our pleasure and delight.

First of all are the collections of complete cars, with most Jalopy Valhallas gravitating to the gasoline cars of a pre-1920 vintage. There are also a few collectors of steam cars and electrics, two vehicles that once challenged gas car supremacy and now as dead as a dodo. Next comes the car insignia collector,—both the name plates sold with the car and the emblems attached to the car by the original owner after purchase. Of the name plates, the earliest ones were inconspicuous brass tags affixed to the dash and bearing serial numbers

Automobile Nameplates from the F. Walker collection

and model identification dates as well as maker's name. As cars came to be widely advertised, the maker's name plate came to be placed where it could be seen by people on the street. The early Oldsmobile had a decalcomania tag on either side of the body near the driver's seat. Pope and Flanders had their script names cut out of sheet brass and attached to the front cooler-pipes. Around 1910 makers began to use distinctive plates in several colors of enamel, affixed to the radiator shell just below the filling cap. In the 1920's name plates left the radiator shell to roost in such new and unaccustomed places as a bar between the head lamps, the gas cap, the bumper, the rear trunk door or as a plug to fill the now unused starting crank hole. The high point of insignia design came in the late 1920's and early '30's, when radiator caps became identifying ornaments. Outstanding examples are the metal knights used by Willys-Knight, the Packard bird and the Lincoln dog. Collectors who cannot secure these elusive radiator ornaments will take hub-caps as second best, for special markings have been placed on these down to the present day. Over and above all this, in terms of rarity and interest, are the emblems and badges that the early car owner attached to his chariot himself. Easiest to acquire are the insignia of such clubs as the A. A. A., next came the badges of early car insurance companies, the fraternal organization designs and finally the gilded ornaments that were sold to doll up the early radiator cores—flies, frogs, dancing girls, Kewpies, in fact most every variety of animal and bird. A state license plate is something in a class by itself. And in all these fields, we think especially of the Swigart collection at Huntington, Pennsylvania. Here indeed is the Emperor of Emblems.

A great deal of collector interest has also been shown in early automotive equipment, especially horns and lights. The big gas searchlights made by Solar, Rushmore and other companies are highly prized. One of these powerful lights was usually mounted near the dash for night driving. Operated on a two-way swivel by the passenger in the front seat, it was swung back and forth over the road to pick out the better

BOBBY NORTH'S TERRIFIC HIT!

HE'D HAVE TO GET UNDER—
GET OUT AND GET UNDER
(TO FIX UP HIS AUTOMOBILE)

WORDS BY
GRANT CLARKE &
EDGAR LESLIE

MUSIC BY
MAURICE ABRAHAMS

MAURICE ABRAHAMS MUSIC CO.
1570 BROADWAY
· NEW YORK

WHALEN & LAROSE

Automobile songs show public reactions of the period. The song covers
reproduced on the following pages are largely from the early 1900's.

parts of the then usually impossible terrain. Next in desirability comes the oil-burning brass side lamps and the later pairs of carbide gas headlamps. The latter were usually extra equipment and cost originally as much as one hundred dollars a pair. As the early 1900 cars had no bumpers and as the headlamps were the first to arrive at a collision point, it is easy to understand why these parts are scarce.

One of the finest collections of auto parts is owned by Alfred Lewerenz of Los Angeles. The alert observer will find collections of old spark plugs, horns, tire tools, in fact any and all old auto parts, springing up in many parts of the country.

Automobile Literature is a fascinating field in itself and, incidentally, the major contributor to this book. Outstanding are the brochures distributed by manufacturers in the early days of industry. Equally treasured are the manuals given to the original purchaser, telling how to operate and repair the car. Back files of the Saturday Evening Post, Harpers and Leslies, and other magazines popular at the turn of the century are valuable. These pictures are frequently consulted by old car enthusiasts to settle an argument as to whether or not an old car belonging to one of them is properly equipped. In a very special class are the early issues of trade magazines; publications such as the Automobile Trade Journal, Motor Age and Horseless Age are scarce as hen's teeth. Automobile book collecting falls into four classes: Manuals on car operation by such authorities as Homan, Pemberton and Page; books telling of thrilling automobile races, early cross country treks and endurance trails; novels built around the doings of a car; and, lastly, books of reminiscences by early auto enthusiasts.

Reading through old catalogues and books on the auto, one can readily appreciate that the definitive history of this man-made creation lies in the future. It has not been attempted herein. For one thing, we are too close to the automobile, still too dependent upon it to have a proper perspective. That will come only at some distant date, when men dart around in rockets and helicopters, when something else has

216

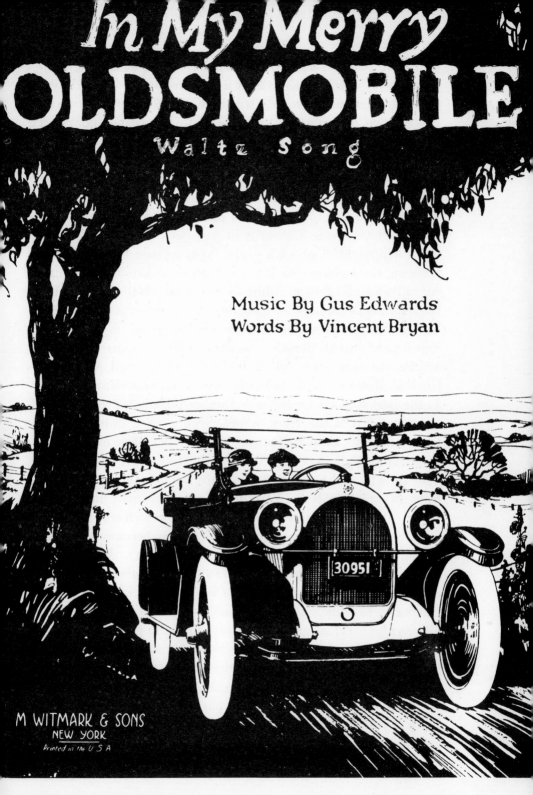

In My Merry OLDSMOBILE

Waltz Song

Music By Gus Edwards
Words By Vincent Bryan

M WITMARK & SONS
NEW YORK
Printed in the U S A

Most popular automobile song of all time. Originally introduced by Gus Edwards, it has gone through innumerable editions, is still a great favorite.

taken the place of our present day necessity, when the automobile will be almost as extinct a creature as the horse-drawn chariot. Then and then only will it be seen for what it truly is.

A great deal more automotive history must be uncovered before this development can be fully assessed. For the benefit of some future historian, we may venture a few questions of emphasis and intent that have not found answers here. Why did the gas buggy win out over the steam car and the electric in popular fancy? Why has the pint-sized car, so popular in Europe, never made a go of it in America? What lies behind the disappearance of such body types as the rear entrance tonneau, the rumble seat job, the victoria cabriolet. Is motor car advance largely a thing of the past, with all possible improvements forecast in trial designs of decades ago? Will Kaiser-Frazer, only new automobile company to make its appearance in two decades, be able to find a place for itself among the now stratified industrial giants, Ford, Chrysler, General Motors? Will the rear-engine automobile, advanced as the post war car by the now tuckered Tucker, ever become a reality? Will the front wheel drive, once a Cord masterpiece and now even disappearing from the Jeep ever get a full trial? Will cars eventually take to wings, a half-way helicopter? And how are we to place the relative accomplishment of pioneers like Kettering, Ford, Durant, Chapin and Olds? Why is the achievement of Durant known only in automotive circles, while the name of Ford has become a symbol for all the bad features of industrial America? Why is the name of Chapin, the man who did so much for good roads, not on the Hudson car he created? Why do we insist in associating R. E. Olds with the Oldsmobile, a company he forsook almost at its formation, and not with the R. E. O., the company he managed for years and the car he said was perfected in 1912 "almost to finality"? What of the early attempts to combine the automobile with the airplane and the motor boat? Will any of these still see the light of popular demand? Those are but a few of the questions that will intrigue the curious reader and stimulate future research.

218

Automobile songs show public reactions of the period. The song covers reproduced on the following pages are largely from the early 1900's.

THE LITTLE FORD RAMBLED RIGHT ALONG

GREATEST COMEDY SONG SENSATION

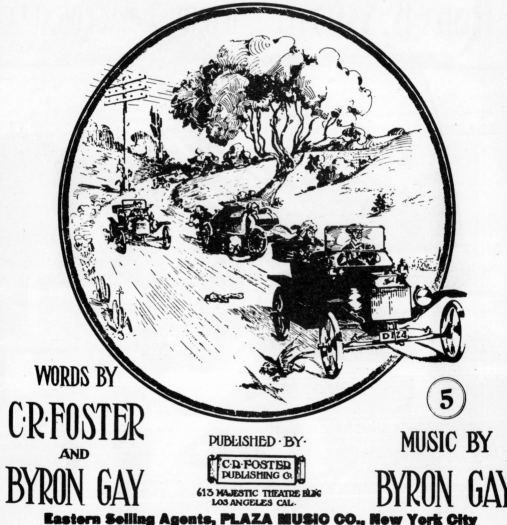

WORDS BY
C·R·FOSTER
AND
BYRON GAY

PUBLISHED·BY·
C·R·FOSTER
PUBLISHING Co.
613 MAJESTIC THEATRE BLDG
LOS ANGELES CAL.

MUSIC BY
BYRON GAY

⑤

Eastern Selling Agents, PLAZA MUSIC CO., New York City

All motor manufacturers hoped for a song that would popularize their own model, and some actually commissioned writers. The Ford, of course was a natural, profited by such hits as the above and The Back Seat of Henry Ford.

All motor manufacturers hoped for a song that would popularize their own model, and some actually commissioned writers.

THE AUTOMOBILE HONEYMOON

As Sung By

LEW DOCKSTADER

WRITTEN BY

HARRY · B · NORRIS ·

5 4/-

Published by JOS. W. STERN & CO 34 EAST 21ST ST. NEW YORK

NEW YORK
CHICAGO

LONDON · PRICE & REYNOLDS

The Lady Chauffeur

Intermezzo

by Arthur Hauk

JOS. MORRIS

TUMBLE IN A RUMBLE

WORDS BY
CHARLES NEWMAN

MUSIC BY
J. FRED COOTS

PUBLISHED BY
MILLER MUSIC
INCORPORATED
62 WEST 45TH STREET N

Typical of the last of the automobile songs, when the novelty was gone.

Our story has dealt mainly with the heartfelt revival of interest in early automobiling days. Led by enthusiastic collectors of old cars, by song revivals and by radio jokes, the "Merry Old Mobiles" are now playing return engagement. It is fun to see the old cars, fun to have one's picture taken at their wheel, fun to hear the honk of an old horn, fun to view a Glidden Tour revival in full swing. As we look at the old cars and read of them, memories return—memories of our own first days with the automobile. We recall all the makes we have owned, those owned by our fathers, our u n c l e s, our friends. We recall experiences had or heard about—fixing tires by the light of the moon, putting up a one-man top while the rest of the family sat drenched by the sudden downpour, having the acetylene headlight fail miles from home, being tried for speeding by a greedy Justice of the Peace, having a horse rear right towards the back seat, being choked with dust while using fence rails to jack up a wheel on some detour, and the time when having a car saved a life. These and countless other memories come back to us as we think about this, our most glorious mode of transportation, a possession more highly prized than the Bedouin's camel, the family car. Time was when anyone who drove could also take his car apart. Thanks to precision engineering, we no longer have to give a car's insides much thought. We step on the electric starter and away we go. In a generation the automobile has grown from a mechanical upstart into a dominant factor in everyday life. We've come a long way in a short time. Is it any wonder we turn back the pages, look over the way we have travelled in the merry old mobiles?

"Maxwell and Stanley and Reo Runabout
Apperson Jackrabbit, Ford's Model T—
Now they're just relics we all laugh about
Time has moved forward, but too rapidly.
Our sleek sedan and our snappy convertible
Give us more stylishness, comfort and speed.
Yes, life is faster, but also less joyable
So we keep memory fresh for this need."

ROLL CALL OF AMERICAN AUTOMOBILES

MANUFACTURED BETWEEN 1895 AND 1950

SURVIVING MAKES ARE PRINTED IN HEAVY TYPE

1908	ABC	1907-1913	Atlas	1916-1923	Birch	
1922	ABC	1900-1936	Auburn	1921-1922	Birmingham	
1909-1916	Abbott		Aultman Steamer	1899	Black	
1917	Abbott-Cleveland	1907	Aurora	1905	Black Crow	
1920-1922	Ace	1903-1922	Austin	1909-1910	Black Crow	
1903-1911	Acme	1930-1935	Austin Bantam	1904	Black Diamond	
1911	Adams	1899	Auto-Acetylene	1902-1905	Blackhawk	
1904-1913	Adams-Farwell	1910	Auto-Bug	1928-1929	Blackhawk	
1921	Adelphia	1899-1911	Autocar	1906	Blakeslee Electric	
1921-1922	Adria	1913	Auto Cycle	1906	Bliss	
1909	Advance	1901	Auto Dynamic	1907-1909	BLM	
	AEC	1900-1901	Automobile Fore	1904-1908	Blomstrom	
	Aero		Carriage	1903	Blood	
1905-1906	Aerocar	1921	Automatic	1901-1906	Boisselot	
1921	Aerotype	1900-1902	Automobile	1901	Bolte	
1901-1903	Ajax Electric		Voiturette	1905	Borbein Electric	
1923-1925	Ajax (Nash)	1901-1904	Automotor	1913-1914	Borland Electric	
1901	Akron	1914	Auto Tricar	1902	Boston and	
1902	Alamobile	1900	Auto Two		Amesbury	
	Aland	1903	Auto Vehicle	1898	Boston Haynes	
1909-1912	Alco		Avery		Apperson	
1910	Aldo	1909-1913	Babcock	1908	Boston High Wheel	
1904-1909	Alden-Sampson	1906-1911	Babcock Electric	1916-1922	Bour-Davis	
1914-1922	Allen	1901	Bachelles Electric	1914	Bournonville	
1907-1909	Allen-Kingston	1905	Bacon	1921-1922	Bowman	
1908	Allith	1911-1912	Badger	1900-1902	Bramwell	
	Alma	1907	Bailey	1899	Bramwell-Robinson	
1910-1914	Alpena	1907-1916	Bailey Electric	1915	Brasie	
1915-1916	All-Steel	1917-1921	Baker Steamer	1902-1904	Brazier	
1920-1921	Alsace	1899-1917	Baker Electric	1902-1903	Brecht Steamer	
1916-1917	Alter		Balboa	1908	Brennan	
1905	Altha Electric	1902-1903	Baldner	1904-1905	Brew & Hatcher	
1921-1922	Ambassador	1900	Baldwin Steamer	1915-1937	Brewster	
1916-1925	American	1902	Ball	1920-1923	Briggs & Stratton	
1905-1914	American	1905	Banker	1912	Brightwood	
1918	American	1914	Bantam	1914-1921	Briscoe	
1912	American	1923	Barbarino	1903	Bristol	
1911	America	1922-1924	Barley	1909-1917	Broc Electric	
1937	**American Bantam**	1922	Barlow Steamer		Brock	
1899-1900	American Electric	1907-1912	Barnes		Brodesser	
1902-1903	American Gas	1896	Barrow Electric	1920-1921	Brook	
1902-1903	American Gas	1901-1903	Bartholomew	1908	Brooks	
1903	American Mercedes	1903	Bates		Brooks Steamer	
1909	American Mors	1914	Bauer	1916	Brown	
1900	American Power	1906-1907	Bay State	1914	Brown	
	Carriage	1922-1926	Bay State		Brown Burtt	
1935	American Steam	1914-1917	Beardsley Electric	1910	Brownell	
	Car		Beaver	1915-1916	Brownie	
1922-1923	American Steamer	1918-1922	Beggs	1908-1910	Brownieker	
1912	American Tri-Car	1907-1911	Belden	1907-1911	Brush	
1912-1915	Ames	1907	Bell	1901	Buckeye	
1898	Ames	1915-1922	Bell	1906-1912	Buckeye	
1908-1915	Amplex	1908	Belmont	1914	Buckles	
1917	Ams-Sterling	1910	Belmont	1903-1907	Buckmobile	
1909	Anchor	1912	Belmont	1900-1907	Buffalo	
1908	Anderson	1916	Belmont Electric	1901-1907	Buffalo Electric	
1916-1926	Anderson	1907	Bendix	1901-1909	Buffum	
1913	Anger	1914	Benham	1908-1909	Buggycar	
1808	Angus	1908-1917	Ben Hur	1907	Bugmobile	
1909	Anhut	1908-1909	Benner	**1903**	**Buick**	

226

1915	Appel	1901	Century Tourist	1921	Commodore
1917	Apple	1905-1912	Chadwick	1917-1922	Commonwealth
1900-1926	Apperson	1906-1912	Chalfant	1904-1906	Compound
1906	Apollo	1908-1923	Chalmers	1901-1903	Conrad
1905-1906	Ardsley	1902	Champion	1909-1912	Continental
1916	Argo	1909-1910	Champion	1914	Continental
1912-1917	Argo Electric	1919-1926	Champion	1907-1908	Continental
1919	Argonne	1899-1901	Chapman Electric	1933-1934	Cont'nental
1906	Ariel	1917	Charter Oak	1903-1912	Corbin
1913	Aristos	1910	Chase	1907-1916	Corbet·
1914	Arrow Cyclecar	1901-1904	Chelsea	1929-1937	Cord
	Artsberger Steamer	**1913**	**Chevrolet**	1922	Corinthian
	Atlantic Electric	1906	Chicago Steamer	1913-1915	Cornelian
1908-1911	Bergdoll	1914-1917	Chicago Electric	1907-1909	Cornish-Friedberg
1904-1911	Berkshire	1906	Chicago	1911-1914	Correja
1906-1909	Berliet	1914-1916	Chicago		Corweg
1908-1912	Bertolet	1908	Chief	1907-1910	Cosmopolitan
1904	Bessemer	1904-1906	Christie	1901	Cotta
1900	Best		Christman	1903	Country Club
1904-1908	Bethelem	**1924**	**Chrysler**	1904-1912	Courier
1904	Beverly	1903	Church	1919-1924	Courier
1915	Bewis	1913	Church	1902-1907	Covert
1916-1922	Biddle	1911-1913	Churchfield Elec-	1920	Craig-Hunt
1915	Biederman		tric	1906-1907	Craig-Toledo
1917 ·	Bimel	1903	Cincinnati Steamer	1912-1914	Crane
1888-1902	Binney and		Cinco	1916-1924	Crane-Simplex
	Bunham	1908-1911	Cino	1902-1924	Crawford
1910	Burg	1901-1912	Clark	1905-1908	Crescent
1910	Burns	1906-1910	Clark Electric	1914-1915	Crescent
1914-1916	Burroughs	1900-1909	Clark Steamer	1913-1915	Cricket
1917-1924	Bus	1900-1908	Clarke-Carter	1902-1904	Crestmobile
1908-1909	Byrider Electric	1908-1909	Clark-Hatfield	1912	Criterion
1902	Cadillac	1903-1906	Clarksmobile		Croesus, Jr.
1912	California		Classic	1903-1905	Crompton
1914	California	1905	Clear and Dunham	**1939**	**Crosley**
	Californian	1912	Cleburne	1899-1900	Crouch
1927	Calvert	1903	Clermont	1901-1903	Crowdus Electric
1905-1907	Cameron	1922	Clermont	1914-1925	Crow-Elkhart
1909-1921	Cameron	1909	Cleveland	1915	Crown
1916-1921	Campbell	1902-1906	Cleveland	1908-1909	Crown
1901	Canda	1919-1926	Cleveland	1915-1917	Crowther-Duryea
1904-1906	Cameron	1919-1923	Climber	1911-1914	Croxton
1906	Cantono Electric	1902-1903	Cloughley	1909-1912	Croxton-Keeton
1902	Capitol Steamer	1911	Club Car	1918	Cruiser
1923	Cardway	1919	Clyde	1923	Crusader
	Carhart	1908	Clymer	1901	Cull
1911	Carhartt	1921-1922	Coats Steamer		Culver
1904-1911	Carlson	1908-1910	Coates-Goshen	1900-1907	Cunningham
1913	Car-Nation	1912	Cogswell		Steamer
1908	Carrison	1906-1911	Colburn		Cunningham
	Carthage	1911-1914	Colby	1910-1912	Cutting
1912-1920	Carrol	1910-1925	Cole	1907	C. V. I.
1920-1922	Carroll		Collinet	1914-1915	Cycleplane
1907-1911	Cartercar	1901	Collins Electric	1923	D. A. C.
1909	Carter Twin	1912	Colonial Electric	1922-1927	Dagmar
	Engine	1917-1921	Colonial	1911	Dalton
1924	Cartermobile	1921-1922	Colonial	1916-1924	Daniels
1909-1927	Case	1908	Colt	1912	Daniels
1907	Cato	1916-1925	Columbia	1911	Dan Patch
	Cavac	1898-1913	Columbia	1909-1910	Darby
1927	Cavalier	1898-1906	Columbia Electric	1917	Darling
1902	Centaur	1916	Columbia Electric	1901-1902	Darling
1905	Central	1903-1906	Columbus	1903	Darrow
1901-1903	Century	1906-1909	Columbus	1922	Dart
1901	Century Steam	1917-1923	Comet	1902-1903	Davenport
1911-1912	Century Electric	1914	Comet	1909-1928	Davis
1917	C-B	1921	Commander	1914	Davis
			Commerce		Dawson

1911-1914 Day	1933 Dymaxton	1902-1903 Fanning
1911 Dayton Electric	1915-1917 Eable Electric	1916 Farmack
1909-1911 Dayton	1905-1906 Eagle	1906-1907 Farmobile
1911 Deal	1908 Eagle	1922-1924 Farner
1902-1903 Decker	1909 Eagle	1907-1909 Federal
1914 De Cross	1914 Eagle	1905 Federal Steamer
1906-1909 Deere	1924 Eagle	1914 Fenton
1918-1919 Deering Magnetic	1917 Eagle Rotary	1920-1923 Fergus
DeLa Vergne	1907-1909 Earl	1920-1923 Ferris
1924-1927 Delling Steamer	1916-1924 Earl	Findley
1923 Delmore	1897 Eastman Electric	1906-1911 Firestone-
1914 Deltal	1898 Eaton Electric	Columbus
1906-1909 De Luxe	1903-1909 Eck	1902-1904 Fisher
1909-1911 Demotcar	1901-1902 Eclipse Steamer	1908 Fish
De Motte	1906 Economy	1902-1904 Fischer
1911 De Rain	1917-1919 Economy	1914 Flagler
1901-1902 Desberon	1914 Economvcar	1911-1912 Flanders
1913 De Soto	1902 Eddy Electric	1914 Flanders Electric
1928 **De Soto**	1912-1914 Edwards-Knight	1904 Flexbi
1909-1912 De Tamble	1902 Eichstaedt	1902-1904 Flint
1912-1915 Detroiter	1916 E.I.M.	1924-1927 Flint
1907-1938 Detroit Electric	1915 Elbert	1913-1914 Flint
1900 Detroit	1908-1930 Elcar	1924-1927 Flint
1916 Detroit	1915-1916 Elco	1913-1914 Flyer
1922 Detroit	1903-1906 Eldredge	**1903** **Ford**
Detroit Steamer	1913 Electa	1908 Forest
1914 Detroit-Speedster	1901 Electronomic	1908-1909 Fort Pitt
1912 Detroit-Chanham	Steamer	1898-1905 Foster Steamer
1909-1910 Detroit-Dearborn	1916-1924 Elgin	1906-1907 Fostoria
1931-1932 Devaux	1903 Elinore	1906 Fostoria
1899 Dewabout	1909-1910 Elite	1921-1925 Fox
Day Electric	1901 Elite Steamer	Frankfort
1905-1911 Diamond T	1908-1911 Elkhart	1902-1934 Franklin
1924-1928 Diana	1899-1902 Elliott	1905-1909 Frayer-Miller
1914-1916 Dile	1901 Ellis Electric	**1947** **Frazer**
1917-1918 Disbrow	Ellsworth	1902-1904 Fredonia
1912-1922 Dispatch	1900-1911 Elmore	1914 Frederickson
1912 Dixie	1909 Elwell-Parker	1922-1923 Fremont
1915-1924 Dixie Flyer	1909 Emancipator	1913 French
1908-1909 Dixie Tourist	1907 Emerson	1900-1903 Friedman
1913-1924 Doble Steam Car	1916-1917 Emerson	1921 Friend
1913-1924 Dodge Steam Car	1909-1912 E. M. F.	1907-1917 Frichie Electric
1914 **Dodge**	1898-1901 Empire	1909-1911 Frontenac
1926 Dodgeson	1910-1919 Empire	1917 Frontenac
1904-1907 Dolson	1922-1923 Endurance Steamer	Frontmobile
1906-1926 Dorris	1901 Englehardt	1915-1917 F. R. P.
1915-1925 Dort	1910-1917 Enger	1912 F. S.
1918-1922 Douglas	1914 Engler	1907-1911 Fuller
1914 Downing	1911 Entyre	1908-1911 Fuller
1913 Downing-Detroit	1914 Entz	1908 Fulton
1906-1908 Dragon	1897 Erie	1911 F. W. D.
1921-1922 Drake	1916-1821 Erie	1912 Fwick
1916-1917 Drexel	1927-1930 Erskine	1910 Gabriel
1921-1923 Driggs	1906-1908 Essex Steamer	1914-1915 Gadabout
1915-1916 Drummond	1919-1932 Essex	1902-1906 Gaeth Steamer
1914 Dudley	Euclid	1906 Gale
1907-1909 Duer	1908 Eureka	1919-1931 Gardner
1921-1934 Duesenberg	1909-1914 Eureka	1907-1913 Garford
1902-1904 Dumont	1907-1909 Evansville	1905-1906 Gas-au-lec
1914-1917 Dunn	1909-1911 Everitt	1901-1903 Gasmobile
1909 Duplex	1908-1909 Everybody's	1911-1912 Gaylord
1915-1923 DuPont	1908-1909 Ewing	1908 Gearless
1903-1906 Duquesne	1917-1918 Fageo	1920 Gearless Steamer
1921-1932 Durant	1909-1911 F. A. L.	1917 Gem
1908-1910 Durocar	1922 Falcon	1903 General
1895-1914 Duryea	1909-1911 Falcon	1899 General Electric
1912 Dusseau	1927-1928 Falcon-Knight	1911-1912 Genesee
1903 Dyke	1909 Famous	1901-1909 Geneva

1902	German-American
1917-1921	Geronimo
1921	Gersix
1918	Ghent
	Gibbs Electric
1899	Gibson
1916	Gillette
1909	G. J. G.
1910-1914	Gleason
1902-1919	Glide
1921-1922	Globe
1921	Glover
	Goethe
1906	Goldeneagle
1922	Goodspeed
1908	Grabowsky
1899	Graham
1927-1930	Graham-Paige
1930	Graham
	Gramm
1912	Grand
1912	Granite Falls
1914-1923	Grant
1899-1903	Graves-Condon
1922-1925	Gray
1911-1914	Great Eagle
1911	Great Smith
1910-1914	Great Southern
1909-1916	Great Western
1903	Greeley
1922	Gregory
1901	Grensfelder
1899-1903	Greuter
1914	Greyhound
1910-1915	Grinnell Electric
1907	Griswold
1906	Grout
1901	Gurley
1014	Gyroscope
1916-1919	Hackett
1918	H. A. L.
1902	Hall
1908-1912	Halladay
1919-1921	Halladay
1908	Hamrock
1917	Hamilton
1920-1921	Hamlin-Holmes
1905	Hammer
1923	Handley
1921-1922	Handley-Knight
1922-1924	Hanover
1902	Hansen
1917-1923	Hanson
1916	Harding
	Hardy
1907	Harper
1925	Harrie
1922	Harrigan
1923	Harris
1904-1907	Harrison
1917-1922	Harroun
1908	Hart-Kraft
1898	Hartleysteamer
	Hartman
1916	Harvard
1900	Hasbrouck
1916	Haseltine
	Hassler

1906-1908	Hatfield
1912-1914	Havers
1907	Hawley
1907-1908	Havberg
	Haydock
1900-1925	Haynes
1895-1900	Haynes-Apperson
	Hayward
1914-1915	Hazard
1920-1926	H. C. S.
1911	Healy Electric
1918	Hebb
1921-1922	Heifner
1908	Heilman
1907	Heine-Velox
	Hendel
1913	Henderson
1922-1930	Henney
1901	Henrietta Steamer
1911	Henry
1902	Hercules
1914	Hurcules
1915	Herff-Brooks
1914	Herreshoff
1895-1898	Hertel
1925	Hertz
1902	Hess Steam
1905-1910	Hewitt
1900	Hewitt Lindstrom
1898-1899	Heyman(n)
1900	Hicks
1922	Highlander
1907-1908	Hill
1908	Hines
1909	Hobbie
1902-1904	Hoffman
1902	Hoffman Steamer
1915	Holden
1905	Holland
1900-1903	Holley
1915	Hollier
1916-1917	Holly
1908	Holmes
1919	Holmes
1902-1906	Holsman
1906-1908	Hol-Ten
1899-1903	Holyoke
1917-1923	Holyoke
1917-1918	Homer Laughlin
1914	Hoosier Scout
1902	Hopkins
1921	Hoskins
	Houghton
1900	Houghton Steamer
1909-1910	Houpt
1910-1912	Houpt-Rockwell
1901-1910	House Steamer
1901	Howard
1903-1905	Howard
1914	Howard
1903	Howey
1909	**Hudson**
1901	Hudson Steamer
1920-1925	Huffman
1921	Hunter
1908	Hupmobile
1914	Hupp-Yeats
	Electric

1917	Hydromotor
1902	Ideal
1903	Ideal
1905	Ideal
1914	Ideal
1909	Ideal Electric
1901	Illinois Electric
1909-1914	Illinois Electric
1914-1915	Imp
1903-1909	Imperial
1908	Imperial
	Imperial Electric
1912	Independence
	Independent
	Indianapolis
1917	Ingrame-Hatch
1921-1922	Innes
1901	International
1900	International Gasoline Carriage
1908-1910	Interstate
1904	Intrepid
1906-1908	Iroquois
1908	Iverson
1902-1921	Jackson
1900	Jacks Runabout
1921	Jaquet
1911	James
1906-1908	Janney
1912	Jarvis-Huntington
1903	Jaxon Steamer
1902-1916	Jeffrey
1922	Jem
1908-1911	Jenkins
1906-1909	Jewel
1923-1927	Jewett
1905-1912	Johnson
1905-1908	Johnson Steamer
1914-1920	Jones
1902-1907	Jones-Corbin
1911	Jonz
1918-1930	Jordon
1914	J. P. L.
1925	Julian
1925	Junior
1947	**Kaiser**
1894-1900	Kane-Jennington
1919	Kankakee
1909	Kansas City
	Kato
1909-1912	Kauffman
1914	K. D.
1908-1916	Kearns
1900-1901	Keene Steamobile
1908-1914	Keeton
1914	Keller Kar
1903	Kellogg Steamer
1902-1924	Kelsey
1912	Kenmore
1915-1918	Kennedy
1899-1903	Kensington Steamer
1917	Kent
1921-1922	Kenworthy
1907	Kermath
	Kermet
1900	Kerosene Motor Surrey

1900 Keystone
1909 Keystone Steamer
1907-1909 Kiblinger
1901 Kidder
1912 Kimball Electric
1905-1922 King
1913 Kinn(e)ar
1903 Kirk
1906-1931 Kissel (Kar)
1923 Kleiber
1911 Kline (Kar)
1907-1909 Klink
1900 Klock
1901-1903 Knickerbocker
1917 Knight Special
1900-1913 Knox
1911-1914 Koehler
1903 Konigslow
Komet
1914 Koppin
1901 Kraft Steamer
1908 Kreuger
1909-1916 K. R. I. T.
1902-1906 Kunz
1921-1923 Kurtz
1900-1907 Laconia
1914 Lad's Car
1920-1923 Lafayette
1934 Lafayette
1919-1920 LeMarne
1905-1917 Lambert
1899-1901 Lancamobile
1899-1905 Lane Steamer
1909-1912 Lanpher
1900-1908 Lansden Electrette
La Petite
1900 Larchmont Steamer
1910 Larson
1927 La Salle
1917-1919 Laurel
1914 Lauth Jergens
1914 L. C. Erbes
1922-1931 L. & E.
1920-1922 Leach-Biltwell
1911 Leader
1908-1909 Lehr
1909 Lende
1916 Lenox
1909 Lenox Electric
1916 Lescina
1899-1901 Lewis
1914-1915 Lewis
1908-1928 Lexington
1916-1925 Liberty
1915 Lima
1908 Lincoln
1914 Lincoln
Lin(d)sley
1914 Lion
1913 Little
Little Mac
1899-1929 Locomobile
1906-1909 Logan
1913-1914 Lomax
1917-1921 Lone Star
Long
Longest
1900-1904 Loomis

1907 Lorraine
1919-1921 Lorraine
1913-1914 Los Angeles
1900 Louisiana
Lowell-American
1901-1902-Lozier Steamer
1901-1916 Lozier
L. P. C.
Lueding Haus
1917 Lutz Steamer
1906-1914 Luverne
Lyman
Lyman-Burnham
1911 Lyon
1914 (Lyons-Knight
(Lyons-Atlas
1906-1909 Maccar
1923 MacDonald Steam
Car
1903 Mackle-Thompson
1917 Macomber
1915-1917 Macon
1916-1918 Madison
1914 Magic
Magnolia
1905 Mahoning
1916 Maibohm
Magestic
1915 Malcolm
1914 Malcolm-Jones
Malden-Steamer
1921 Manevall
1912 Manistee
1908 Maplebay
1908-1918 Marathon
1902-1905 Marble Swift
1910-1914 Marion
1916-1917 Marion-Handley
Mark Electric
1900-1902 Marlboro Steamer
1904-1933 Marmon
1912 Marquette
1930 Marquette
1903-1914 Marr
1898-1899 Marsh
1920 Marsh
1919-1920 Marshall
1920 Martin
1926-1931 Martin
1920 Martin-Wasp
1907 Marvel
1900 Maryland
1906 Mason
1898 Mason Steamer
Massilon
Master
1903-1913 Matheson
1907-1908 Mathews
1908-1909 Maxim-Goodridge
Electric
1910-1925 Maxwell
1904-1910 Maxwell-Brisco
1899 Mayer
1925 Mayfair
1911 Maytag
1909 McCue
1899 McCullough
1919 McCurdy

1912-1927 McFarlan
1922 McGill
1904-1915 McIntyre
1900-1902 McKay Steamer
1912 Mead
1916 Mecca
1907-1908 Med-Bow
1900-1907 Media
1923 Mel Special
1908 Menges
1910-1925 Mercer
1904 Mercury
1918 Mercury
1939 Mercury
1922 Merit
1905-1906 Merkel
1914 Merz
1902-1903 Meteor Steamer
1903-1908 Meteor Steamer
1914-1921 Meteor Steamer
1914 Metropol(e)
1922 Metropolitan
1909-1921 Metz
1912 Metzger
1909 Michigan
1909-1913 Middleby
Midg'ey
1908-1909 Midland
Midwest
1908-1909 Mier
1913-1914 Mighty Michigan
1916 Milac
1914-1922 Milburn Electric
Militaire
1912-1913 Miller
1900-1902 Milwaukee Steamer
1915 Minneapolis
1914 Mino
1903-1922 Mitchell
Mitchell-Lewis
1899-1902 Mobile Steamer
1903-1906 Model
1909 Modoc
Mogul
1903-1904 Mohawk
1903-1904 Moline
1908 Moline
1914-1920 Mol'ne-Knight
1921 Moller
1917 Monarch
1908 Monarch
1901 Moncrief(f)
1914 Mondex-Magic
1916 Monitor
1916 Monroe
1900-1903 Moody
1900 Mooers
1905-1930 Moon
1906-1907 Moore
1916-1921 Moore
1906-1909 Mora
1914 Morgan
1922 Morris-London
1895-1897 Morris & Salom
Morris(s)
1904-1909 Morse
1914-1917 Morse
1906 Motorette

1903-1904	Moyea	1914-1915	O-We-Go	1903-1909	Pope-Toledo
1911-1915	Moyer	1905-1906	Oxford	1904-1906	Pope-Tribune
1915-1916	M. P. M.	1914	Pacific	1903-1907	Pope-Waverly
1895	Mueller-Benz	**1899**	**Packard**	1917	Poppy-Car
1922	Mulford	1907	Page	1921-1922	Porter
1913-1914	Multiplex	1910	Page-Teledo	1922	Port Huron
1906	Muncie	1909-1927	Paige	1900	Porter Steamer
1905	Murdaugh	1909-1927	Paige-Detroit	1914	Portland
1902-1903	Murray	1906	Palmer	1907-1908	Postal
1921	Murray-(Mac)	1905	Palmer-Moore	1909-1912	Power-Car
	Mutual	1907-1914	Palmer-Singer	1920-1922	Prado
1912-1913	Nance	1918-1922	Pan	1912-1914	Pratt-Elkhart
1909	Napier	1902-1904	Pan-Am	1903-1927	Premier
1916	Napoleon	1917-1922	Pan-American	1922	Premocar
1918	**Nash**	1909	Panther	1922	Preston
1900-1924	National	1905-1907	Paragon	1900-1905	Prescott Steamer
	National Electric	1922	Paragon	1914	Pridemore
	Neilson	1920-1922	Parenti	1906-1915	Primo
1903-1904	Moyer	1909-1911	Parry	1917	Princess
1918-1921	Nelson	1905	Parsons-Electric	1902	Prospect
1903	Neustadt-Perry	1914-1917	Partin-Palmer	1907-1925	Pullman
	Newark	1913-1917	Pathfinder	1902-1910	Pungs-Finch
1899-1900	New England	1908-1924	Paterson	1902	Puritan Steamer
	Steamer		Paterson-	1902-1906	Queen
1916-1917	New Era		Greenfield	1899-1900	Quick
1901	New Home	1901-1902	Pawtucker	1909	Rae
1907-1928	New York		Steamer	1914	Railsbach
1903-1905	Niagara	1906-1909	Payne-Modern	1904-1910	Rainier
1915-1916	Niagara	1900-1932	Peerless	1921-1922	Raleigh
	Nichols Shepard	1911-1913	Penn	1902-1914	Rambler
1902	Noble	1916-1919	Pennsy	1905	Randall
1919-1924	Noma	1907-1911	Pennsylvania		Randall Steamer
1903-1906	Northern	1901	People's	1910	Randolph
1921-1922	Northway	1906-1908	Perfection	1907	Ranger
1904	Northwestern	1913	Perfex	1920-1922	Ranger
1902	Norton		Peru	1899-1903	Rap'd
1917	Novara	1913	P. E. T.	1905-1917	Rauch & Lang
1911-1922	Norwalk	1914-1916	Peter Pan		Electric
	Underslung	1921-1922	Peters	1922-1928	Raulang Electric
1912-1914	Nyberg	1908-1911	Petrel	1911-1914	Rayfield
1917-1932	Oakland	1917-1919	Phianna	1912--1916	R-C-H
	Oakman-Hertel	1903	Phelps	1914	Read
1915	Obertine	1911-1913	Phipps Electric	1900-1902	Reading Steamer
1916-1922	Ogren	1900	Phoenix	1912	Reading
1917-1921	Ohio Electric	1908-1912	Pickard		Real
1909-1915	Ohio Electric	1917-1922	Piedmont	1902-1903	Reber
1911-1913	Ohio Falls	1901-1938	Pierce Arrow	1928	Red Bug
1902-1908	Okey	1906	Pierce-Racine		Red Jacket
1917-1922	Oldfield	1916	Pilgrim	1921	Rees
1898	**Oldsmobile**	1916	Pilliod	1908	Reeves
1917-19-8	Olympian	1909-1924	Pilot	1908-1922	Regal
1913	Omaha	1909-1914	Pioneer	1903-1905	Regas
1909-1915	Only	1901	Piscorski	1902	Reinertsen
1901	Orient	1909-1912	Pittsburgh	1908-1909	Reliable Dayton
1904-1905	Ormond Steamer	1896-1899	Pittsburg Electric	1905	Reliance
1911-1914	Orson	1906-1909	Planche	1923	Remal-Vincent
1911	Otto	1910	Plymouth		Steamer
1903-1904	Ottoker	**1928**	**Plymouth**	1901-1914	Remington
1911-1912	Ottomobile	1914	Pneumobile	1903-1936	Reo
1903-1905	Overland	1902	Pomeroy	1912-1916	Republic
1906-1939	Overland	1922-1926	Pomeroy	1919-1926	Re Vere
1912	Overholt	1916-1923	Ponder	1914	Rex
1899-1900	Overman Steamer	1902-1908	Pontiac	1908-1909	Rhodes
1910-1914	Owen	**1925**	**Pontiac**	1914-1920	Ri Chard
1915-1921	Owen Magnetic		Pope	1922	Richelieu
1915-1916	Owen Shoeneck	1895-1912	Pope-Hartford	1905-1914	Richmond
	Owen Thomas	1902-1904	Pope-Robinson	1922-1927	Rickenbacker

1909 Ricketts
1916 Riddle
1909-1911 Rider-Lewis
1922 Reiss-Royal
1899 Riker Electric
1902 Riley & Cowley
    Steamer
1917 Riper
1914 Ritz
    Riveria
1911 R-O
1911-1912 Roader
1916-1929 Roamer
    Robe
1914 Robie
1900-1902 Robinson
1912 Robson
    Roche
1901 Rochester Steamer
1902 Rockway
1913-1914 Rocket
1919-1925 Rock Falls
1931-1933 Rockne
1908-1912 Rockwell
1921 Rodgers
    Roebling
1895 Rogers
1911-1912 Rogers
1899 Rogers Steamobile
1902 Rogers & Hanford
1923-1925 Rollin
1921-1936 Rolls Royce
1909 Roman
1921 Romer
1928-1929 Roosevelt
1899 Roper Steamer
1905-1909 Ross Steamer
1905-1917 Ross
1904-1905 Rotary
1922 Rotary
    Rovena
1904-1910 Royal
1904-1911 Royal-Tourist
1922-1924 Rubay
1918 Rush
1902 Rushmobile
1902-1903 Russell
1929-1930 Ruxton
1920-1925 R & V Knight
1914-1916 Saginaw
1912 Salter
1904-1911 Sampson
1903 Sandusky
1902-1904 Santos Dumont
1912 Savage
1914-1922 Saxon
1907-1924 Sayers
1905-1913 Schacht
1901 Scott
    Scott-Newcomb
    Steamer
1915-1922 Scripps-Booth
1901 Seagrave
1901-1903 Searchmont
1909-1913 Sears
1910 Sebring
1923 Sekine
1903-1912 Seldon

1909-1912 Sellers
1906-1910 Senator
1917-1924 Seneca
1915 Serpentina
1921 Serrifile
1908-1909 Seven Little
    Buffaloes
1920-1922 Severin
1912-1916 S. G. V.
1917-1919 Shad-wyck
1902-1903 Shain
1915-1916 Sharon
1908-1909 Sharp-Arrow
1905 Shaum
1914-1921 Shaw
1905-1910 Shawmut
1902-1903 Shelby
1921 Sheridan
1906-1909 Shoemaker
1911 Sibley
1912 Sibley-Curtis
1913 Signet
1912 Silent
1908-1909 Silent Knight
    Silver Knight
1920 Simms
1907-1914 Simplex
1907-1920 Simplicity
1907-1909 Simplicity
1908-1909 Simplo
1915-1920 Singer
1906 Single Center
1900-1904 Sintz
1915-1916 S. J. R.
1920-1922 Skelton
1900 Skene Steamer
1913-1914 S & M
1904-1907 Smith & Mabley
    Simplex
1921 S-N
1906-1908 Snyder
1908-1914 Sommer
1905-1908 Soules
1921-1922 Southern
1907 Sovereign
1920 Spacke
    Spartan
1902-1903 Spaulding
1910-1916 Spaulding
1909-1910 Special
1905-1906 Speedway
1907-1909 Speedwell
1901 Spencer Steamer
1921-1922 Spencer
1921-1923 Sterling
1914-1917 Sphynx
1908-1916 Spoerer
1904-1906 Springer
1908 Springfield
1914 Sprite Cyclecar
1899 Squier Steamer
1917 S.S.E.
1912-1914 Stafford
1905 Stammobile
    Steamer
1900 Standard Steamer
1921 Standard Steamer

1916-1922 Standard-8
1902 Standard
1915 Standard
1904-1905 Standard
1909-1910 Standard
1912-1914 Standard
    Electrique
1908-1909 Stanley
1912 Stanley
1896-1925 Stanley Steamer
1899 Stanley Whitney
1901 Stanton Steamer
1921-1922 Stanwood
1908 Star
1922-1928 Star
    Starin
1917-1919 States
1923 Static Super
1907-1914 Staver
1901-1902 Steamobile
1898 Stearns Steam
1899-1912 Stearns
1912-1930 Stearns-Knight
1914-1916 Steco
1907-1908 Steel Swallow
1908 Steinhart Jensen
    Steinmetz
1916-1924 Stephens
1909-1915 Sterling
1914-1916 Sterling
1916-1925 Sterling Knight
1917 Stetson
1915-1916 Stewart
1922 Stewart-Coates
1902-1927 Stevens-Duryea
1913-1914 Stickney-Motorette
1908-1909 Stilson
1909 St. Joe
1899-1901 St. Louis
1899-1907 St. Louis
1911 Stoddard
1904-1913 Stoddard-Dayton
1902 Storck
1915 Storms Electric
1935 Stout Scarab
1909 Stratton
1899-1901 Strathmore
    Steamer
1909 Stratton
1908 Streator
1901 Stringer Steamer
1910 Strobe & Martin
1915 Strouse
1903 **Studebaker**
1905-1910 Studebaker-
    Garford
1902-1904 Studebaker Electric
1898 Sturgis Electric
1904-1908 Sturdevant
1913-1935 Stutz
1911-1912 Stuyvesant
1912 Suburban
1906 Success
1906-1911 Sultan
    Summit
1918-1922 Sun
1906-1909 Sunset
1914 Superior

232

1922	Supreme	
1904-1908	Synnestvedt	
1899	Syracuse Electric	
1922-1923	Tarkington	
1901-1904	Taunton Steamer	
1918-1924	Templar	
1910	Templeton-Dubrie	
1915	Tex	
1918-1921	Texan	
	Texmobile	
1902-1912	Thomas	
1906-1908	Thomas-Detroit	
1901-1904	Thompson	
1901	Thorobred	
1900	Thresher Electric	
1913	Tiffany	
	Tiffin	
1914	Tiger	
1904-1909	Tincher	
1899	Tinkham	
1900-1903	Toledo Steamer	
	Tonawanda	
1902-1908	Torbensen	
1914-1916	Touraine	
1902-1909	Tourist	
1906	Traveler	
1910-1914	Traveler	
1907	Trebert	
1913-1914	Tribune	
	Trimo	
1901	Trimoto	
1900	Trinity Steamer	
1900-1909	Triumph	
1914-1915	Trumbull	
1918-1922	Tulsa	
1912	Twincity	
1911-1915	Twombly	
1902-1908	Twyford	
1902-1909	Union	
1912	United	
1917	Universal	
1903-1905	Upton	
1908	U. S.	
1899-1901	U. S. Electric	
1900-1904	U.S. Long Distance	
1909	Van	
1911	Van-L	
1912	Van Dyke	
1900	Van Wagoner	
1905	Vaughn	
1914	Vaughn	
1923	Vaughn	
1903-1904	V. E.	
1908-1928	Velie	
1916-1922	Vernon	
1914	Vestal	
1900-1902	Victor Steamer	
1908-1909	Victor	
1913-1914	Victory	
1920-1921	Victory	
1929-1930	Viking	
1908	Viking	
1914	Vixen	
1917-1923	Vogue	
1914	Voiturette	
1913-1915	Vulcan	
1915-1917	Waco	

1913-1915	Wagenthals	
1914	Wahl	
1909-1910	Waldron	
1905-1906	Walker	
1901-1904	Walls	
1906-1909	Walter	
1920-1922	Waltham	
1900-1909	Waltham Orient	
1903	Walther	
1905	Walworth	
1914	Ward	
1914	Ward Electric	
1909-1914	Warren	
1901	Warwick	
1908-1923	Washington	
1907	Washington	
1909-1911	Washington	
1919-1925	Wasp	
	Waterloo	
1906	Watrous	
1910	Watt	
1908	Waukesha	
1898-1916	Waverly-Electric	
1904-1909	Wayne	
1904-1911	Welch	
1912-1925	Westcott	
1912	W. F. S.	
1900	Whaley-Henriette	
1902	Westfield	
1921-1922	Wharton	
1926-1930	Whippett	
1910-1920	White	
1902-1910	White Steamer	
1906	White Hickory	
	White Star	
1911-1912	Whiting	
1878-1899	Whitney Steamer	
1902	Wick	
1909-1911	Wilcox	
1902	Wildman	
1907	Williams Electric	
1921-1926	Wills-Sainte Claire	
1908	**Willys-Overland**	
1914-1932	Willys-Knight	
1928-1930	Windsor	
1922	Wing	
1920-1921	Winther	
1897-1924	Winton	
1921-1922	Wizard	
1902-1907	Wolfe	
1904-1906	Wolverine	
1917-1918	Wolverine	
1927-1928	Wolverine	
1917	Wonder	
1902	Woodruff	
1900-1917	Woods	
1917	Woods Duel Power	
1914-1918	Woods Mobilette	
1900-1910	Worth	
1903-1904	Yale	
1917	Yale	
	Yates	
1905-1908	York	
1902-1907	Zent	
	Zentmobile	
1908-1916	Zimmerman	
1913-1914	Zip	

1909-1910	Burdick
1902-1903	Berg
	Anthony

THE OCTOAUTO

AN APPRECIATION BY ELBERT HUBBARD

¶ In the good old days when I used to take cattle to the Chicago Stock Yards, I carried a long hickory pole, a basket of grub, and much enthusiasm.

¶ On long runs, my home was in the caboose for perhaps three days and three nights. It was a sad day, however, when, instead of a regular, genuine caboose, they bundled the merry stockmen into a dinkey.

¶ The difference between a dinkey and a caboose is that a caboose has four wheels on each side, and a dinkey has only four wheels altogether, one on each corner. The dinkey's business is to bounce, jounce, jolt, jar and jerk, and make a puncture in your vocabulary.

¶ A wheel is a plan of continually hitting the rail. The Pullmans, it was, who discovered that when you hit the rail in twelve places in running a car, you greatly reduce the amount of jar and the wear and tear both on the rails and the rolling-stock.

¶ A car having twelve wheels is considered doubly as safe as one having eight.

¶ A wheel lives its life exactly as a man does his. A man will stand a great number of raps and kicks supplied by Fate, provided they are distributed over a long period of time, but when you come to concentrate them in a few years, or a few months, or a few days, you destroy the man by destroying his nerve fabric.

¶ In the Reeves Octoauto, the load is distributed over eight wheels, instead of being concentrated on four. In a four-wheeled automobile, a wheel at each corner carries one-fourth of the load. In case of an imperfection in the road, the sudden dropping down into a rut, one wheel may for an instant carry half of the load, and it is this sudden jolt and burden that causes the tire trouble. You get enough of these tremendous pressures in a day, and your tire reaches its limit and explodes with a loud R. G. Dun and Company report. If you are running fast, you may lose control and the ditch, always waiting, gets you. So the proposition is, if you can save your wheels from these severe jolts which will occasionally come through dropping into a rut, you are going to prolong the life of the tire, the life of the car and the life of its occupants.

It's Styled to Stay Beautiful— and Engineered to Stay New!

Here's thrifty driving at its finest ...at the wheel of Plymouth's Finest! Plymouth is low-slung, long, wide and roomy...with a wonderfully smooth new ride. Advanced engineering makes it your *Wise Buy!*

Plymouth's Finest has great power as well as grand style...a full 95 horsepower...power you can afford because of great new driving economy! The big, eager Plymouth engine breezes along with fewer revolutions per mile ...reduces wear...saves gas.

The smart Convertible Coupe has the famous power-operated top...full-width red leather seat cushions, front and rear.

See your nearby Plymouth dealer. All prices and specifications subject to change without notice. PLYMOUTH DIVISION OF CHRYSLER CORPORATION.

The handsome new Station Wagon comes in either two-tone or natural finish body.

Buy Wisely—Buy PLYMOUTH

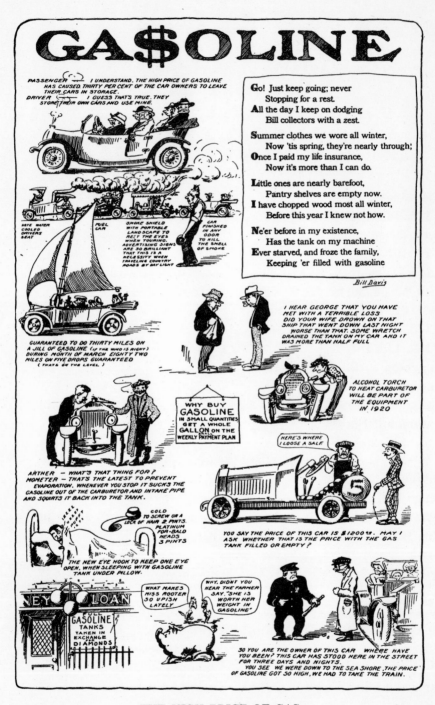

THE HIGH PRICE OF GAS
Throughout all decades, this has been a recurrent subject of cartoon comment.

Index

239

THE END